The Johns Hopkins University Digital Portfolio and Guide

Documenting Your Professional Growth

The Johns Hopkins University
Center for Technology in Education

Upper Saddle River, New Jersey
Columbus, Ohio

Vice President and Executive Publisher: Jeffery W. Johnston
Assistant Editor: Ben M. Stephen
Production Editor: JoEllen Gohr
Design Coordinator: Diane C. Lorenzo
Cover Designer: Ali Mohrman
Cover image: Fotosearch
Production Manager: Pamela D. Bennett
Director of Marketing: Ann Castel Davis
Marketing Manager: Darcy Betts Prybella
Marketing Coordinator: Tyra Poole

This book was printed and bound by R. R. Donnelley & Sons Company. The cover was printed by Phoenix Color Corp.

Pearson Prentice Hall™ is a trademark of Pearson Education, Inc.
Pearson® is a registered trademark of Pearson plc
Prentice Hall® is a registered trademark of Pearson Education, Inc.
Merrill® is a registered trademark of Pearson Education, Inc.

Pearson Education Ltd.   Pearson Education Australia Pty. Limited
Pearson Education Singapore Pte. Ltd.   Pearson Education North Asia Ltd.
Pearson Education Canada, Ltd.   Pearson Educación de Mexico, S.A. de C.V.
Pearson Education—Japan   Pearson Education Malaysia Pte. Ltd.

10 9 8 7 6 5 4 3 2 1
ISBN: 0-13-171323-X

Preface

Portfolio Development and Use at Johns Hopkins University

The Graduate Division of Education within Johns Hopkins University (JHU) is a national leader in the development and use of portfolios for pre-service teachers. Beginning in the early 1990s, the University's Master of Arts in Teaching (MAT) program required its pre-service teachers to develop a portfolio in lieu of a master's thesis. Over time, the required portfolio evolved from a collection of artifacts illustrating examples of program components to a reflective synthesis of the teacher candidate's growth and mastery of national standards for beginning teachers.

The portfolio development process requires teacher candidates to collect examples of their work during their internship and other field experiences. After selecting exemplary evidence of their successes, candidates develop a narrative reflection that links the selected evidence to standards. [In the MAT program at Johns Hopkins University, the Interstate New Teacher Assessment and Support Consortium (INTASC) standards are used.] Portfolios typically contain artifacts (such as lesson and unit plans, student work, and photographs) along with associated interpretations, rationales, and reflections.

In 2001, Johns Hopkins University transitioned from a paper-based portfolio to a digital portfolio. This new system allowed teacher candidates to seamlessly integrate multimedia and other digital evidence into their portfolios. It also provided a means for them to demonstrate mastery of new technology skill requirements: both technical skills (such as scanning, editing, and uploading documents) and instructional skills (that is, the ways they integrate technology into the lessons they create and deliver).

Throughout the portfolio development process at Johns Hopkins, faculty and staff provide support related to the content and technical aspects of portfolio development. Pre-service teachers have opportunities to receive input from advisors, other trusted faculty, and peers as they refine their portfolios. Presentation of the portfolio to a faculty panel is the culminating event of the MAT program. Following completion and presentation, the portfolio becomes valuable to graduates in their job search. For those educators who choose to continue to build their professional portfolios, the JHU Digital Portfolio can also be used to document professional growth, to seek new positions, and to provide evidence needed to obtain promotions and advanced certifications.

The JHU Digital Portfolio has been widely used over the last three years, with thousands of recent graduates and in-service professionals using it to document and present their pre-service accomplishments. These students and faculty have embraced the digital portfolio and recognize the limitations of a cumbersome and inflexible paper-based format. Given the institution's very positive experiences with the JHU Digital Portfolio, Johns Hopkins University is pleased to have the opportunity to share this resource with other colleges, universities, and organizations that provide pre-service education and professional development to teachers.

The Johns Hopkins University Digital Portfolio and Guide

The Johns Hopkins University Digital Portfolio is an electronic repository of a student's work organized around a defined set of professional principles/standards. It allows for collection and display of artifacts, such as:

- Lesson plans
- Audio and video clips
- Sample student work
- Other Web-based materials
- An online journal for reflection
- A messaging system promoting collaboration with peers and advisors

This accompanying guide contains your access code for registration (see inside front cover) for the JHU Digital Portfolio, as well as practical, how-to instructions for using the JHU Digital Portfolio System to create your own digital portfolio.

Organization of the JHU Digital Portfolio Guide

The guide is divided into two parts. The first part begins by introducing students to portfolio development and the importance of reflection throughout the process. The discussion then moves to the specific elements unique to the JHU Digital Portfolio. Part II presents a step-by-step user's guide for the JHU Digital Portfolio, including guidance and practical tips for constructing your digital portfolio.

Special Features of the JHU Digital Portfolio Guide

- **Discussion Questions.** Thought-provoking questions at the end of Chapters 1–3 can be used during in-class discussion or for individual response.

- **Activities.** Located in Chapters 1–3, these are opportunities to practice and apply what you are reading.

- **Quick Clicks.** Woven throughout Part II of this guide, these include succinct step-by-step instructions for developing your digital portfolio.

Intended Audiences for the JHU Digital Portfolio Guide

This guide is primarily intended as a resource for pre- and in-service teachers and for teacher educators.

For Pre- and In-service Teachers

For One Course. Teachers will use this guide as they conceptualize a portfolio, gather artifacts that provide evidence of what they have learned in this course, and reflect on and construct their portfolio entries. The information in this guide will be useful in each phase of portfolio development as it addresses conceptual, technical, and procedural issues.

Across Multiple Experiences. This guide may also be useful to educators who want to use the JHU Digital Portfolio System to develop a comprehensive portfolio that encompasses many courses or activities.

For pre-service teachers, this would likely include artifacts from all of their field experiences. For in-service teachers, a portfolio might include materials from multiple professional development experiences, materials that might be useful in obtaining a new position, or materials that document their attainment of specific competencies required for promotion or advanced certification.

For Teacher Educators

Teacher educators and professional developers will find that this guide provides background information related to the varied uses and critical elements of portfolios as well as how-to information needed to design and assemble a digital portfolio. In particular, this guide explains how the JHU Digital Portfolio can be used for a single course or an entire program and how the application can be customized to the particular standards that are most relevant to the purpose for and context of its use.

Features of the JHU Digital Portfolio

- **A Web-based environment with a user-friendly interface** allows users to access and input information easily from any computer with Internet access. Whether in their dorm room, or in class, or in a student teaching experience, users can easily add, share, and revise content; send or receive materials for assessment; and access a comprehensive help function.

- **A File Cabinet feature** allows users to easily add artifacts and files to their working portfolio. Similar to a traditional filing cabinet, the JHU Digital Portfolio File Cabinet offers a tool for uploading, storing, and organizing a wide variety of electronic files for later inclusion in a student's portfolio. Transition from collection and annotation to presentation is accomplished in one simple step.

- **The standards are determined by the school or program** and provide the primary organizational structure for the students' portfolios (INTASC, ATE, ISTE, CEC, NCTM, etc.). INTASC standards are pre-loaded. In addition, students can easily input their own sets of local, state, or national standards relevant to their area of expertise.

- **The JHU Digital Portfolio reinforces and encourages reflective teaching practice** through a convenient journal tool. Space is provided for recording and storing reflections and thoughts about professional experiences. The Journal tool allows for conversion of entries to artifacts in order to help demonstrate growth over time.

- **Final presentation portfolios** serve as both a showcase of student work for prospective employers and a vehicle for continued professional development and reflection. Students can produce multiple Web-based portfolio presentations simultaneously, tailored for specific uses (completion of a course, an education program, or for employment).

- **A built-in Message Center** provides a communications hub from which messages and feedback may be sent and received from one easy-to-use, convenient interface for the purpose of constructive feedback. This feature encourages and facilitates collaboration by furnishing students with an easy, safe, and secure method for sharing their work with peers, advisors, and a portfolio review team.

Technical Requirements

The JHU Digital Portfolio is a Web-based application, accessible from any computer with Internet access. Because the JHU Digital Portfolio is Web-based, it works with both PC and Mac platforms. Although users may prefer the faster access available through a broadband Internet connection, the application is designed to run on a 56K modem connection. As a Web browser, we recommend using at least Netscape Version 7, Internet Explorer 6 (or higher) or Mozilla Firefox. We recommend that you disable any pop-up blockers before launching the Digital Portfolio application.

System requirements: Windows 95 or better; Macintosh or power Macintosh, OS 9.0 or better.

Acknowledgments

For the last decade, students and faculty from the Masters of Arts in Teaching (M.A.T.) program within the Johns Hopkins University School of Professional Studies in Business and Education (JHU SPSBE) have been at the forefront of the practice of using portfolios as a mechanism for reflection, a dynamic record of professional development, and as a summative instrument demonstrating learning and achievement. Currently the Dean of SPSBE, and formerly the Director of the Graduate Division of Education, Dr. Ralph Fessler has provided the philosophical direction and strong leadership that guides all aspects of our work in teacher preparation. The faculty that comprise the M.A.T. program, particularly Drs. Teresa Field, Elaine Stotko, and Angelique Renee Johnson, continue to forge new ground in the effective use of portfolios in teacher education, continually improving and refining the process based on experience and research.

In 2000, the task of transforming a well-established, effective, paper-based portfolio process into something new that harnessed the power of multimedia and the Internet fell to the Johns Hopkins Center for Technology in Education (CTE). Thanks largely to several grants from the U.S. Department of Education, CTE was able to lead a comprehensive effort to match the cumulative knowledge gained from years of using portfolios with the latest in secure Web application development technologies. Dr. Jacqueline Nunn, CTE's Director, along with Betsy Lowry and Dave Peloff, led CTE's work in developing the digital portfolio system, which is now the centerpiece of multiple degree programs at Johns Hopkins. CTE also thanks James Hagen and Alex Markson from the firm NoInc for their strong graphic design and programming assistance.

The writing of this guide was a team effort, representing the work and ideas of many distinguished educators and researchers whose vision helped guide the development of the Johns Hopkins Digital Portfolio system. Part I (Chapters 1–3), which focuses on the pedagogical nature of portfolios and effective implementation strategies, was written and edited (in alphabetical order) by Gigi Devanney, Dr. Teresa Field, Randy Hansen, Betsy Lowry, Richard Messick, Dr. Jacqueline Nunn, Elaine Peirrel, and Dave Peloff. Part II (Chapters 4–6), which is more of a specific "how-to" manual for using the Johns Hopkins Digital Portfolio system, was written and edited by Gigi Devanney, Randy Hansen, and Richard Messick.

Forged over the past eighteen months, the partnership between Johns Hopkins University and Merrill Education has been strong, professional, and collegial. The complexities of forging a relationship between organizations from academic and commercial sectors can be daunting, but the resulting partnership arrangement has been extremely positive and mutually beneficial. A true collaboration, this project would never have reached fruition without the vision and perseverance of the Merrill Education team including publisher Jeff Johnston, and the dedicated work of Ben Stephen, Darcy Betts, Dan Parker, JoEllen Gohr, and others.

In addition, we are grateful for the suggestions of the following reviewers: Gail Dickinson, Old Dominion University; James D. Lehman, Purdue University; and Ivan Wallace, East Carolina University.

JOHNS HOPKINS UNIVERSITY
Center for Technology in Education
School of Professional Studies in
Business and Education

Contents

Part I

The Teaching Portfolio

Chapter 1

The Teaching Portfolio: Purposes and Elements

The use of portfolios in teacher preparation programs has become quite common over the past decade. If you are reading this book, it is likely you are creating or soon will be creating your own portfolio. This chapter offers information on the theory behind portfolios and provides an introduction to some elements that are commonly incorporated into them.

Concept of Professional Portfolios

The concept of the professional portfolio originated in occupations where creativity is essential. Employers seeking to fill positions in jobs related to art, advertising, and journalism have long required submission or review of a portfolio during the hiring process. In recent years, the use of portfolios has expanded into other fields, as it has been recognized that a well-conceived and well-executed portfolio can help document achievements and skills in virtually any field.

A teaching portfolio, like an artist's portfolio, is a collection of work that illustrates an individual's talents as an educator (Doolittle, 1994). Teaching is a highly complex combination of specialized knowledge, skills, and dispositions (Martin-Kneip, 1999), and demonstrating competency as an educator requires careful thought and consideration. A teaching portfolio allows educators to show what they are capable of doing through artifacts that demonstrate both pedagogical skills and content knowledge as measured against a common set of principles or standards.

It is important to understand that the body of work collected and assembled into a portfolio is not merely a collection of lesson plans, student assessments, or notes home to parents. Creating a portfolio involves careful selection and reflection on the part of the educator. It requires the educator to delve deeper to examine and describe his or her reasons for entering the field of education, explain a philosophy about teaching and learning, and articulate career goals.

Portfolios are not static. Portfolios can be used to help teachers document and examine their current practice, as well as help them set goals that will lead to improvement in their work (Martin-Kneip, 1999). Over time, educators' portfolios will develop and change as they become more accomplished and work in a variety of contexts (Edgerton, Hutchings, & Quinlan, 1991). The hallmark of the teaching portfolio is the thoughtful inclusion of reflection. The topic of reflection will be explored in more detail later, however, it is important to note that *"Reflection is key to improving both teaching and learning, at the core of becoming an effective educator"* (Valli, 1992).

Types of Teaching Portfolios

Portfolios can be used for a variety of purposes. While containing common elements, each type of portfolio is developed for a different audience that requires the tailoring of materials and content to a specific purpose. The four types of portfolios discussed in this book are the pre-service teaching portfolio, the employment portfolio, the professional development portfolio, and the promotion or National Board certification portfolio. Regardless of the type of portfolio, developers must collect, select, and reflect upon evidence that demonstrates who they are as educators.

Pre-service Teaching Portfolio

The original version of the JHU Digital Portfolio was developed for use in pre-service programs to assess teacher candidates' progress toward meeting program standards. The pre-service teaching portfolio provides an opportunity for aspiring teachers to demonstrate that they have met the identified standards through their coursework and field experiences.

Employment Portfolio

An employment portfolio can be used by recent graduates, career-changers seeking to enter the field of education, and in-service teachers who are interested in obtaining a new position. This type of portfolio uses a blend of the individual's educational philosophy and the job's requirements as a framework for portfolio contents.

Professional Development Portfolio

This type of portfolio is created by an educator to track progress toward individual professional goals. It may include documentation of college and university coursework, professional development courses, and other career-related activities. A professional development portfolio provides evidence of the educator's accomplishments, which can be shared with supervisors who are responsible for observing and documenting teacher performance.

Promotion/Advanced Certification Portfolio

This type of portfolio, like the pre-service teacher portfolio, uses standards to guide the development and reflections of an accomplished and experienced teacher. However, this portfolio demonstrates growth over a teaching career, not just the relatively short period of the typical pre-service internship. These portfolios are also characterized by richer and more extensive artifacts and by a higher level of reflection.

Each portfolio (pre-service, employment, professional development, and promotion) addresses a specific need for evaluating and assessing personal and professional growth based upon a set of standards or goals. Some elements of one type of portfolio may be useful in another, but the artifacts with reflections will likely increase in number and complexity as the educator gains experience.

Digital Portfolios: Benefits and Use

Making changes to the traditional paper portfolio was time-consuming and cumbersome, since it was typically assembled in large binders using plastic page protectors. Also, the students were rarely able to share their work with colleagues as the single copy was passed from one instructor to another for the review process. Finally, after a quick evaluation by program faculty, the paper portfolio was returned to the student who probably filed it away and forgot about it. As computers began to take over the business sector, the limitations of this process became more evident.

Generally, teacher education programs have been slower to adopt technology than other fields of study. In many institutions, the U.S. Department of Education's Preparing Tomorrow's Teachers to Use Technology Program (PT3) was the catalyst for many teacher education programs to fully embrace technology. As a result, many teacher education programs began to see value in digital rather than paper-based portfolios. Instructors began to see new opportunities for the continued and expanded use of a digital portfolio that could follow a student from undergraduate school to a teaching position, on to graduate school, and throughout his or her career.

Include a Variety of Media

Electronic portfolios overcome the limitations of paper-based portfolios because the developer can document his achievements with a variety of media beyond text and photographs. The incorporation of a rich array of media makes a portfolio more interesting for reviewers, as well as allows them to see how effectively the pre-service teacher interacts with students, manages the classroom, and conveys content knowledge.

Accessibility

Publishing a portfolio on the Web allows an unlimited number of people to review it, which is especially beneficial during the formal review. Faculty and other reviewers do not have to share a single copy, allowing them to review the portfolio in virtually any setting, at a time that suits their individual schedules, and in greater depth. (CD-ROM/DVD publication allows for multiple copies to be produced and distributed relatively easily and inexpensively.)

Flexibility

A digital portfolio, unlike the static and linear paper-based portfolio, allows the developer to move and recombine artifacts quickly and easily. It is also quite possible to include an artifact in more than one section if it clearly illustrates competency related to two or more standards.

Allows for Building and Demonstrating Technology Skills

As technology resources in schools have increased dramatically over the past decade, it has become very important for teachers to have the technology skills needed to use these tools effectively. Many teacher preparation programs have added technical and technology integration skills to graduation requirements. The process of building a digital portfolio supports the development of certain technical skills such as creating, scanning, editing, and uploading documents. It also allows pre- and in-service teachers to include materials that they have used in the classroom and to demonstrate their use of technology in the classroom through digital photos and video.

Activity 1.1: How Do You Rate Your Technology Skills?

Although the JHU Digital Portfolio system requires minimal technology skills—e-mail, word processing, and Web-surfing—as a digital portfolio developer, you may want to review each section of the checklist and note the skills that you already possess. If you have questions about any of the skills described, leave the corresponding box unchecked. After completing the checklist, use it as a guide to determine the areas in which you may need further training or assistance.

Fundamentals

	Start up and shut down a computer
	Log in and out of a computer
	Use the mouse to point, click, double-click, and drag
	Use the right and left button on a mouse
	Identify and navigate within various parts of the desktop: Taskbar, Start Menu, Icons
	Identify parts of a computer system including keyboard, monitor, CPU, mouse, speakers, printer, ports, disk drive, CD-ROM drive
	Open, move, resize, scroll, and navigate within a Window
	Open a program

	Move between two or more Windows
	Use Help including online resources
	Identify and use Windows Explorer (Safari on *Apple*)
	Copy, move, paste, and rename files, folders, and icons
	Create and use Shortcuts
	Select and use a printer

Telecommunications—E-Mail

	Open your e-mail application
	Identify and use the Menu Bar, Shortcuts, and Standard Toolbar
	Use the Folder List and Preview Pane features
	Compose and send an e-mail message
	Reply to and Forward an e-mail
	Send an e-mail with an attachment
	Retrieve an attachment

Telecommunications—World Wide Web: *Internet Explorer*

	Open browser (*Internet Explorer, Netscape Navigator, Mozilla Firefox*)
	Access a specific Web site by entering the appropriate URL in the Address Bar
	Identify and use the buttons on the Standard Toolbar
	Create and use a Favorite
	Use Help, including online resources
	Conduct a simple search using a search engine such as Google

Word Processing

	Open your word processing application
	Type text in a document
	Identify and move the cursor
	Use the cursor to insert text

	Save a document
	Use Help and online resources
	Identify and use the Menu Bar
	Identify and use the Standard and Formatting Toolbars
	Select, drag, move, cut, copy, and past text
	Format a document using bold, italics, and underline
	Format a document using justification, margins, and tabs
	Format a document using numbering and bulleting
	Use the Undo feature
	Print a document

Video and Image Capture

	Use a digital camera
	Put still images into a photo-editing application
	Manipulate still images through cropping
	Save images in various formats and file sizes
	Insert image file into document
	Record images using a digital video camera
	Perform basic video editing
	Edit a video image
	Save a video file

Adaptable and Modifiable

The flexibility of a digital portfolio gives developers the ability to adapt and change their portfolio over time as they gain experience as educators, unlike the more cumbersome paper-based portfolio. The specific standards being addressed may change over time (for example, from INTASC to National Board Certification standards), but an excellent lesson plan may continue to have value as a portfolio artifact regardless of the standards used to organize the portfolio. Because the artifacts are digital, they should last indefinitely and can be easily incorporated into a new portfolio for a new purpose.

Two Approaches to Digital Portfolio Development

There are two general approaches to digital portfolio development. One requires the portfolio developer to create the framework as well as the artifact, known as the common tools method; the second provides a flexible and comprehensive ready-made framework to which the developer adds artifacts and other appropriate content.

Common Tools Software for the Portfolio Framework

Most early digital portfolio development efforts involved use of readily available common tools software, and this practice continues today in many colleges and universities. Pre-service teachers are typically provided with some sort of template or set of guidelines and then use a combination of these available applications to create a digital portfolio. Types of applications frequently used to create the portfolio framework include: relational databases (e.g., Access), hypermedia software (e.g., HyperStudio), multimedia authoring software (e.g., Macromedia Director), Web page creation software (e.g., FrontPage), multimedia slideshows (e.g., PowerPoint), and portable document creation software (e.g., Adobe Acrobat). Regardless of the tools chosen to create the shell or template, students typically use a range of other applications and peripherals to create artifacts or to transform them to digital format. These additional tools and peripheral hardware devices include word processors, image creation and editing software, digital cameras and camcorders, and scanners.

A Ready–Made, Comprehensive Portfolio Framework

The common tools approach described above has the benefit of using software that is generally available at colleges and universities as well as in pK–12 schools. However, the process of creating a portfolio from the ground up using these tools often requires the portfolio developer to master computer graphic design and Web development skills.

Consequently, this process can be quite time consuming and tends to detract from the real reason for creating a portfolio—that is, to demonstrate competency on a set of standards, principles, or goals. Additionally, many of the common tools have a steep learning curve for the user, which also distracts the portfolio developer from his primary task. When provided with a complete portfolio template as opposed to the "portfolio from scratch" approach, the developer is able to devote more time and energy to the value of the portfolio artifacts and reflections. Although they are available from a number of sources and differ in form and style and user interface, a portfolio system is a focused software application that provides the user with a framework for the portfolio. In short, a portfolio system allows users to focus on the development of quality portfolio content without the distractions of learning a new Web-development application or developing significant graphic design skills.

 *Discussion Questions*

1. Why would an employer prefer to see a job candidate's portfolio rather than a résumé?

2. Have you ever kept a journal? What are some of the potential benefits of keeping a journal? Have you ever shared your journal with a colleague or a friend? Why or why not?

3. How could you use a portfolio to tell a story about your experiences?

4. What are the advantages and disadvantages of using common tools software to develop a digital portfolio? What are the advantages and disadvantages of using a digital portfolio application?

5. Looking five years into the future, what could be some potential benefits for developing a digital portfolio?

Chapter 2

Reflection as an Essential Component of the Teaching Portfolio

There is a set of elements that typically comprises a teaching portfolio.

- A statement of the educator's background, educational philosophy, and goals.

- An organizing framework consisting of a set of standards or principles.

- The educator's interpretation of each standard or principle in the framework.

- Documentation (or evidence) of the educator's competencies in the form of artifacts.

   - Artifacts are pieces or collections of evidence that, taken together, help to demonstrate attainment of a standard, principle, or goal.

   - Rationales are reflective narratives about the authentic evidence (artifacts) that provide insight into what the educator learned as well as information about the educational context.

The following elements are often included as evidence:

- Unit/lesson plans and accompanying documents (such as teacher presentations, worksheets, and assessments)

- Examples of student work

- Observations by supervisors

- Photographs

- Video and audio segments (usually limited to electronic portfolios)

In addition, certain types of documents that include reflections can also be used as artifacts in the portfolio. (Note that this is distinct from the reflections in the rationale for the artifact.) These reflections can be in many forms, including:

- Journal entries

- Weekly reflections

- Case studies

- Action research project

In each area of the teaching portfolio noted above, the teacher's critical reflection on each artifact or group of artifacts is essential to the development of a rich and comprehensive picture of a teacher's work. But why is reflection significant and what exactly is a good reflection?

Reflections provide evidence that a teacher is a critical thinker, problem solver, and lifelong learner. John Dewey pointed out the importance of reflection in teaching in the 1930s, noting that "Experience + Reflection = Learning," and belief in the value of teacher reflection continues. Therefore, reflection on practice is essential to educators' professional growth and is at the core of the portfolio development process.

Based on this understanding, reflection has been increasingly integrated in recent years into programs for both pre-service and in-service teachers. It is a critical element of many innovations in teacher development, including case analysis, action research, and portfolio development.

Experts' Views on the Value and Effects of Teacher Reflection

Today, researchers are looking at the value of critical reflection for both new and experienced teachers and are examining how reflection affects the teaching and learning process. Following are some highlights from this growing body of work:

- Self-knowledge is key to successful and meaningful goal setting and career development, and honest critical reflection is the starting point (Lankard, 1996).

- Reflection is not an innate skill possessed by all those in the teaching profession, nor is it uniformly achieved (Baratz-Snowden, 1995).

- An empowered teacher is a reflective decision maker who finds joy in learning and in investigating the teaching/learning process (Fosnot, 1989).

- Reflection is key to improving both teaching and learning, at the core of becoming an effective educator (Valli, 1992).

- While experience in the classroom is an important factor, it is reflection, not experience alone, that is found to be our teacher (Garmston, 2001).

- Critical reflection creates new knowledge constructions and behaviors by blending experience with theoretical and technical learning (Stein, 2000).

- Critical reflection on teaching and learning supports the process of lifelong learning and continuous improvement as an educator (Rodriguez & Sjostrom, 1998).

- Critical reflection is more than acquisition of new knowledge; it is also a questioning of current perspectives, values, and assumptions (Cranton, 1996).

- Reflection is inquiry into pedagogy and curriculum, the underlying assumptions and consequences of educators' actions, and the moral implications of these actions in the structure of schooling (Liston & Zeichner, 1991).

- Reflection is more than "just thinking hard about what you do." Reflective practitioners give careful attention to their experiences, and they analyze the influence of context and how it shapes human behavior (Bullough & Gitlin, 1995).

- Reflection is not about a single event in time, but occurs over time as teachers begin to construct meaning for themselves (Clarke, 1995).

- Becoming reflective involves an active commitment to going beyond routine behaviors and patterns. It's an ongoing commitment to growth, change, and improvement (Brubacher, Case, & Reagan, 1994).

How Portfolio Development Supports Reflection

Developing a portfolio helps educators become more reflective because it provides an opportunity for extensive practice in a highly structured and supportive environment. For a complete and rich picture of the teacher through the view of the teaching portfolio, it is the reflection that allows the viewer to see the artifacts and elements of the portfolio through the teacher's eyes. It is only through the reflection that the portfolio developer can communicate the context, historical and cultural biases, and lessons learned that may have influenced the development or implementation of an artifact.

Reflection Is Required

Most portfolios, including the JHU Digital Portfolio, call for extensive informal and formal reflection at various points and on various levels. The goal is that, through practice, educators will build a habit of mind (Marzano, 1992) to reflect on their practice. Ideally, the foundation for ongoing reflection and self-assessment is laid during the pre-service years, because practicing educators often find it hard to take time for reflection.

Reflection Is Highly Structured

Portfolios require that educators select teaching experiences and artifacts, and develop narratives that describe and explain those experiences. Strong guidelines are provided to portfolio developers about how reflection should be infused throughout the portfolio and the specific elements that should be included in their formal reflections or rationales. (Guidance on developing rationales for the JHU Digital Portfolio is included in Chapter 3.)

Reflections Are Scrutinized and Reviewed by Expert Educators

Graduating reflective practitioners is a primary aim of exemplary teacher education programs. Reflection in a narrative form begins, in most programs, with the application essay and ends with the development and presentation of a teaching portfolio. Between these bookend events there are numerous opportunities for pre-service teachers to reflect upon their teaching and to receive feedback from university faculty and master teachers. (As described in Chapter 3, the JHU Digital Portfolio facilitates provision of this feedback through its collaboration tools.)

Activity 2.1: Narrative Writing

Think about a problematic issue or activity in your own learning or from something you have read for class. The issue might concern a peer or instructor interaction, an instructional event, or a philosophical discourse between your personal beliefs and the research you have read. Please reflect on this issue and write a narrative of your thoughts.

Levels of Reflection

Reflections include written statements that provide insight into an educator's growth. A critical reflection should include information about the background and beliefs of the educator, details of the teaching event encountered, and how this experience affected the way the educator will approach similar events in the future. Ideally, all reflection is critical reflection, but reflection is a habit of mind that must be honed and developed over time.

Arrington and Field (2001) describe three levels of reflection: technical, contextual, and critical. These levels are developmental, and initial studies show that not every educator will progress through the levels to reach the highest level, critical reflection.

Technical

Reflection at the technical level focuses on the refinement of teaching strategies. Typically, educators reflecting at this level describe specific instructional problems only from their own perspective, and do not connect to context; indicate that some instructional problems are more important than others, but do not explain why; focus on finding solutions without considering broader consequences; and are concerned primarily with the efficient and effective application of theoretical knowledge.

Contextual

Reflective practitioners working at the contextual level concentrate on the relationship between the problematic situation and their actions. Typically, educators reflecting at this level situate multiple issues in the classroom or school environment; use a problem-solving process to analyze and reframe important issues to gain greater insight into teaching; are aware of student and faculty perceptions and are sensitive to their needs; explain the use of theoretical and personal knowledge in practical and short-term actions; and consider positive and negative consequences of their actions and accept responsibility for the choices made.

Critical

The reflections of practitioners working at the critical level exhibit deep contemplation and commitment to social justice. Typically, these educators examine classroom issues in relation to knowledge of the wider society; examine issues from multiple perspectives (e.g., teacher, student, parent, administration, community members); propose and prioritize actions in relation to ethical, moral, and caring outcomes; view themselves as change agents and advocates for students, parents, colleagues, and the wider community; and contrast positive and negative long-term consequences for their actions.

As previously noted, not all teachers—even experienced teachers—consistently reflect at the higher levels.

This brief reflection prepared by an intern working in a first grade classroom provides an example of a higher-level reflection by a pre-service teacher.

At six and seven years old, children are so malleable as they attempt to make sense of themselves and their world. Thus, my vision for a unit on poetry centered upon students writing about matters of the heart. First grade students uncovered what they really cared about by creating maps of their hearts, which included: people and places that are important to them; happy and sad memories that have remained in their heart; things they love to do. This enabled the students to visualize their innermost feelings. Once they began to write poetry, I was amazed by the students' ability to access their feelings as well as communicate deep emotions through writing. Through the use of heart maps, I was able to stretch my first graders beyond what many think is possible. This unit invited young children to participate in a process of introspection, whereby they articulated their personal and emotional values and shared their vision with peers through oral reading. I feel that sharing and positive feedback is essential to the social development and self-esteem of students at all grade levels.

Here is another example of a reflection from a pre-service teacher about a goal-setting activity.

I believe that good teachers provide students with opportunities for self-assessment and goal setting. Moreover, when teachers deeply involve students in the process of evaluating their own work, it builds a positive self-concept and motivates them to produce quality work. In first grade, I have addressed the needs of each of my students through the publishing process. By tapping into their prior knowledge and valuing student approximations, I have seen the importance of questioning students so that they will eventually question themselves and self-monitor their own progress. For example, I might ask, "What can you do now that you couldn't do before?" Although I was unable to publish student work as consistently as desired, our conferencing and goal setting did produce positive results. Students in my fourth grade math class also participated in goal setting and conferencing. They wrote about their strengths, their goals, what they enjoy most about math, and what they wish to change.

Levels of Reflection

Level I: Technical Level—Focus on refining teaching strategies

- ◆ Describes specific instructional problems only from own perspective—doesn't connect to context nor prioritize importance

- ◆ Indicates that some instructional problems are more important than others, but doesn't explain why

- ◆ Focuses on finding answers without considering consequences

- ◆ Is concerned with effective and efficient application of theoretical knowledge

- ◆ Considers own teaching performance with assistance of peers but does not propose viable actions or foresee future consequences

Level II: Contextual Level—Focus on relationship between problematic situation and actions

- Situates multiple issues in classroom and/or school environment

- Uses a problem-solving process to analyze and reframe important issues to gain greater insight into teaching

- Notes awareness of student and faculty perceptions and sensitivity to their needs

- Explains use of theoretical and personal knowledge in practical and short-term actions

- Considers positive and negative consequences for actions and accepts responsibility for choices

Level III: Critical Level—Focus on commitment to social justice concerns

- Examines classroom issues in relation to knowledge of the wider society

- Examines issues from multiple perspectives (e.g., teacher, student, parent, administration, community members)

- Proposes and prioritizes actions in relation to ethical, moral, and caring outcomes

- Views self as a change agent and advocate for students, parents, colleagues, and the wider community

- Contrasts negative and positive consequences for various feasible long-term actions

Developed by Arrington & Field, 2001. Reprinted by permission of Angelique Renee Johnson. (Based on Rodriguez & Sjostrom, 1998; McNergney & Herbert, 1997; Ross, 1987; Schön, 1987; Zeichner, 1983; Cruickshank, 1981; Van Manen, 1977; Kolb 1984)

Activity 2.2: Rating Your Level of Reflection

What is your level of reflection on the narrative you have completed thus far? How will knowing the criteria for the levels of reflection assist you in becoming a more reflective educator? Consider the levels of reflection. Look at the reflection you developed in Activity 2.1 and rate it using the Levels of Reflection.

The Collaborative Nature of Reflection

The opportunity to share thoughts, feelings and experiences about teaching with colleagues and friends is important in becoming a more reflective practitioner. Feedback, comments, and discussion about your reflections might come from your mentor or supervising teachers, your university supervisor/coordinator, and your peers in the program. Reflection, as a method of inquiry into teaching, can be collaborative. For example, questions from a friend can help clarify an issue for you, just as a probe or comment from a university supervisor can help you look deeper into the situation or consider another perspective. Collaboration, when developing a portfolio, includes requesting feedback from your mentor, university supervisor, or colleagues and peers. It can also take the form of discussions with colleagues who will assist you in identifying appropriate artifacts or help you in clarifying your beliefs and dispositions.

Activity 2.3: Sharing Your Reflection with Colleagues

Sharing and receiving critical feedback of your personal reflections with colleagues can help you gain a new perspective on a teaching and learning event as well as begin a dialogue that can continue as you develop your portfolio. Critical comments from a colleague during the sharing process can help you clarify your writing as well as help you explore your feelings and reactions to related events.

Share the reflection you wrote in Activity 2.2 with a colleague. In turn, you will review a colleague's reflection. As a reviewer, consider the writing style, the context of the issue discussed, and the level of the reflection. Discuss with the writer your reactions and suggestions for deepening the reflection.

When you are on the receiving end of commentary about your reflection, consider the reviewer's comments as suggestions for improvement and as a way to deepen the level of your reflection. Remember, becoming a reflective practitioner is a learned skill and only through the practice of examining and re-examining your actions can you become truly reflective in your teaching and learning.

Making Time for Reflection

As a student and later as a working professional, it is sometimes difficult to find the time to develop a rich reflection of teaching practices. However, reflection is such a powerful tool for learning, it cannot be an afterthought. Reflection forces you to revisit and rethink your teaching practices and activities and look at your work from other perspectives. The reflections/assignments developed for you have been structured in such a way as to move you through a continuum of reflective thought. (For example, think about your own traits and experiences as a learner before you think about your classroom teaching experiences.) It is important to set aside time each day to process and reflect upon an event, interaction, or issue that is confounding you. It is through this reflective process that you will become an effective educator and a reflective practitioner.

Discussion Questions

1. What are the three levels of reflection and how are they different?

2. Reread one of the teacher reflections included in this chapter. Would you classify the reflection as technical, contextual, or critical? Why?

3. Why is it important to talk about your teaching experience with a colleague or supervisor?

Chapter 3

Planning a Digital Portfolio

This chapter presents information to help you plan your portfolio using the JHU Digital Portfolio System. The information in this chapter is related to the earlier discussed conceptual issues of portfolio development. Subsequent chapters will address technical issues and provide step-by-step guidance on using the portfolio application.

First Steps in Planning a Portfolio

Before beginning to develop a portfolio, the portfolio developer should decide on two fundamentals.

The Purpose for the Portfolio

As previously discussed, portfolios may be used for varied purposes and at various stages in a teacher's career. More specifically, the JHU Digital Portfolio can be used to develop a pre-service, employment, professional development, or promotion portfolio.

The Standards Used to Organize the Portfolio

A useful feature of the JHU Digital Portfolio System is that it can accommodate any set of standards of goals required in a particular circumstance. Standards that might be used to structure the portfolio include:

- Outcomes for a specific course or professional development experience

- INTASC principles

- State Teacher Education standards

- National Board for Professional Teaching standards (NBPTS)

- National Technology Standards (ISTE)

- Standards set by professional associations. (Most content areas, as well as elementary and early childhood areas, have professional organizations that have developed teacher standards for content and pedagogical knowledge.)

- Individual professional goals

This last item warrants some explanation. In addition to recognized standards set by teacher preparation programs, professional associations, and other organizations, the JHU Digital Portfolio can be used to document and track progress on professional goals set by an individual portfolio developer. If this option is chosen, it will be important to give careful thought to the set of goals developed to ensure that they are comprehensive and at an appropriate level of specificity.

The digital portfolio application that accompanies this book allows for the inclusion of course objectives, program standards, or personal goals. Additionally, you might have two sets of standards addressed in your portfolio—one set to assess course objectives, another to track mastery of program standards. When additional standard sets are added this area may be expanded as needed.

Activity 3.1: Linking Your Teaching and Learning to Goals and Objectives

---

Review the objectives or goals that guide your work. These might be content area standards, technology integration standards, or the objectives for a course. Identify one course objective or goal. With a partner, brainstorm ways you could show you have mastered this goal. If someone asked you to "prove" that you had accomplished a goal by showing him a tangible item, how would you do that?

For example, you are taking a PE course on "Running for Fitness." One of the goals of the course is for each student to run at least 10 miles a week and to also complete a 5K run by the end of the semester. Your "evidence" of meeting the weekly running goal could be a runner's log and a map of your daily route. To demonstrate mastery of the second goal of completing a 5K run, you could include a picture of yourself crossing the finish line, a copy of your race registration, and a copy of the final race results.

Portfolio Development as an Iterative Process

A portfolio offers the opportunity to provide evidence in various forms, which collectively demonstrates that the portfolio developer has met a given set of educational standards. Various items (including lesson plans, examples of student work, photographs, and video clips) can be used as portfolio artifacts. Artifacts must be chosen carefully. They must also be accompanied by reflections that give them meaning and link them clearly to the standards that are being used to organize the portfolio. Whatever the purpose or audience for the portfolio, the developer must always be mindful that a portfolio is more than a collection of evidence—more than lesson plans, photos, and examples of student work. A strong articulation of the connection between the artifacts included and each standard or goal is absolutely essential.

Each standard or goal used to organize the portfolio should have at least one artifact, and most should include two or even three artifacts. In many portfolio applications, the portfolio developer is asked to prepare a personal interpretation of each standard or goal. The artifacts, then, should relate not only to the standard as stated, but also to the portfolio developer's understanding of it. An important element of each artifact is the developer's rationale for including it. This rationale should demonstrate the developer's ability to reflect, analyze, and make connections to the standard or goal with which it is associated.

Overall, the process of creating portfolio artifacts is an iterative one. First the portfolio developer collects, on an ongoing basis, all of the items that might possibly be of use. In reviewing the growing collection, the portfolio developer reflects on the array of items, thinking about what is meaningful and why. After selecting one or more items, the developer reflects more deeply and prepares a narrative reflection, which includes a rationale that links and interprets the items. At this point—when items have been selected and a narrative reflection has been developed—an artifact has been created. The explanation of why the items were selected and what they mean make up the rationale.

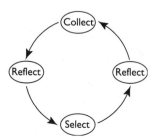

Figure 1.1 The Iterative Process

Collect

It is important to begin collecting potential artifacts as soon as possible. This means saving (electronically, if possible) anything that may ultimately have value as a portfolio artifact. (An extensive list of items to consider and collect appears later in this chapter.)

It is important to be systematic about the collection process. A large file box is useful for hard copy items that may eventually be scanned for the portfolio. As the collection grows, it is a good idea to set up folders for the various categories of items collected. For items created electronically, these should be stored in a separate folder on the developer's computer. Developers should also give thought to creating a backup folder on a CD-ROM, DVD, or external hard drive, as well as online in the JHU Digital Portfolio File Cabinet. Often, student work is included in portfolios, and since most work is not submitted electronically, the developer should scan or copy any student work that may be included in the portfolio before returning it to students. (Keep in mind that all identifying information about students should be removed or covered before being included in the portfolio.) It is advised to obtain permission from students and their parents to use student work samples.

Activity 3.2: Experiencing the Process

Look in your purse, pocket, or briefcase and consider the items you see. Now select one item that holds special meaning for you and put it on the table in front of you. Develop a brief explanation for why that particular item provides an important insight about you.

What you have just done is to identify artifacts—items that represent you in a specific context. Your explanation of these items is your rationale for selecting these artifacts. Artifacts and the accompanying rationale in your portfolio will demonstrate your accomplishment of a specific educational standard.

Reflect

As items are gathered, the portfolio developer will initially look broadly at the array of items, reflect on the collection as a whole, and determine how the individual pieces fit together. At this point, the developer tries to answer questions such as:

- What kinds of things do I have?
- Which pieces best represent my skills and abilities in relationship to the standards I must meet?

At this stage, the emphasis is on the mental process of reflection. But as you develop your portfolio, you might take a few notes concerning what you have collected and the results of the initial review of the items. Developing a list of the artifacts collected, with notations as to where they might be used in the portfolio, will help in keeping track of the growing collection. In some cases, a single item may have utility in more than one section of the portfolio because it is related to more than one organizing standard.

Select

Once the developer has a rich collection of items that might serve as evidence of competencies and accomplishments, it is time to select artifacts that address specific standards or goals. During the artifact selection process, the portfolio developer should be guided by the question: "What evidence do I have that will show someone else that I have mastered that goal or met that standard?"

In reviewing the collection, it is important to understand that an artifact is not necessarily a single item. It is often a small collection of items (such as a lesson plan, student handout, and student work), which, taken together, can be used to demonstrate competency on a particular standard or goal. For example, a developer might want to show her ability to adapt instruction to meet student needs. The portfolio artifact might consist of initial student work that is of low quality, written comments or a journal entry concerning the work, a lesson plan developed to address the specific needs of the struggling student, and another example of student work that shows improvement. Together, these pieces could be considered a single artifact showing evidence of meeting a specific standard.

It is worth noting here that no decision is necessarily final. Until presented, the portfolio is a work in progress. You may initially select items and then, upon further thought, decide that another item or collection of items would be more suitable.

Reflect Again

Once the artifacts have been identified, the most important part of the process begins. The portfolio developer must reflect on the individual pieces that comprise the artifact and carefully consider how the selected items collectively provide evidence on a particular standard or goal. Formal reflections developed to explain the artifact as a whole and justify its inclusion in the portfolio are known as rationales. Rationales should contain four elements:

1. Identification of the artifact components

2. A description of the instructional context

3. An explanation of the instructional purpose and how the various components of the artifact contributed to achieving that purpose

4. A description of student participation and performance during the featured event

Rationales should be concise, but of sufficient length to provide the reader with a clear understanding of how the artifact addresses the identified standard or goal. Depending upon the purpose for the portfolio and instructor requirements, rationales generally range in length from one to three paragraphs.

Major Categories of Portfolio Evidence

There are three major categories of evidence that are typically included in a teaching portfolio: (1) authentic evidence or documentation, (2) explanations and reflections, and (3) validation entries such as observations.

Authentic Evidence or Documentation

These items are examples of the things that the portfolio developer actually did. Examples of this type of evidence are lessons developed and implemented, graded student work (such as tests and essays), parent newsletters about classroom happenings, photos and description of classroom learning stations, and student work products. Much of the evidence will be text-based, although photographs and videotape segments can be used to capture classroom events such as cooperative learning, the use of particular instructional strategies or materials (such as mathematics manipulatives), and student presentations. Most of the evidence in a portfolio is likely to be authentic evidence as it is at the core of artifact creation.* Additional examples are provided below.

Concrete examples of authentic evidence:

- Lesson and unit plans
- Teacher-developed materials, including student handouts
- Student work
- Photos and video clips of classroom activities
- Field trip plans
- Evidence of communications with parents (such as parent newsletters and telephone logs)
- Examples of using technology with students
- Classroom management strategies
- Examples of differentiation of instruction or adaptations for students with special needs
- Assessment instruments (including tests, writing prompts, and rubrics)
- Descriptions of classroom management strategies
- Behavior management plans and contracts

---

* In some cases, when the JHU Digital Portfolio is being used for a single course, there may be little or no opportunity to show the application of knowledge in a field setting. In these cases, coursework, projects, and reflections can serve as evidence of mastery, and the rationales provide opportunities for critical reflection and synthesis of knowledge.

Explanations and Reflections

These include teacher-developed narratives that provide context for and clarification of the authentic evidence in the artifact. In most, cases, there will be a formal rationale developed for each artifact. These may be supplemented by more informal reflections such as journal entries related to a particular incident or even notes jotted at the bottom of a lesson plan about modifications for next time. In some cases, reflections may come from other activities that required reflection; for example case studies and action research projects typically include a reflective component. Cumulatively, these should demonstrate that the portfolio developer is thinking about his or her work and learning from the experiences and the reflective process.

Validation Entries

This type of entry consists of a third-party view of an event or product. Obvious examples are formal observations and evaluations by supervisors. The important thing about a validation entry is that the information is being provided by someone other than the portfolio developer. In essence, another party is providing verification that the identified artifact was of high quality. Validation entries are particularly useful where artifacts include classroom instruction or other classroom activities; even when a videotape segment is included, it will capture only a small part of the event, so having an outside opinion is particularly helpful to reviewers.

Activity 3.3: Identifying and Categorizing Artifacts

Label these artifacts according to the following three categories: Authentic, Reflective, or Validating. Many of the artifacts listed could fit into more than one category, depending upon your rationale for selecting it.

- Teacher-developed plans and materials
- Student work with captions or reflections
- Personal reflections
- Direct observations
- Photos with captions
- Communications with parents, parent volunteer programs
- Educational philosophy

- Telephone logs
- Workshop/Grad course attendance, implementation of the new knowledge, and personal reflection
- Use of technology
- Case studies—your notes, documentation, reflections and examples of student work for one child where you have identified intervention strategies
- Classroom management strategies
- Unit plans
- Photos, video clips
- Action research project
- Field trip plans
- Differentiation/Adaptations
- Examples of different assessment methods
- Special needs modifications
- Behavior management plans/strategies/contracts
- Teacher-developed resources: handouts, graphic organizers, etc.

Providing a Context for the Portfolio

The core of a portfolio is its artifacts. However, to help the reviewer understand the broad context and provide perspective on the artifacts, there are several other important elements included in the JHU Digital Portfolio. These are accessed from the home page and provide an overview of the portfolio developer's background and experiences (including the context in which the portfolio's artifacts were accumulated), a statement of the developer's educational philosophy, and the developer's plans for professional development.

Introduction to You, the Portfolio Developer

This introduction should include a résumé, a description of the settings in which portfolio evidence was accumulated, and other background information that will help a reviewer better understand the portfolio contents.

Résumé

The résumé, which may be embedded or linked to the portfolio, should provide information about educational background and work experiences, especially those that demonstrate teaching or other experiences with children and teenagers. The résumé may be organized according to either a chronological or skill-based format, but the focus should be on providing an organized record of the portfolio developer's experiences as they relate to teaching in pK–12 schools.

Description of Settings

Typically, the résumé will include a two-paragraph description of the settings in which teaching experience has been gained. The first paragraph should provide an overview of the schools (including student demographics), and the second paragraph should describe the classroom settings in which the experience was gained.

Educational Philosophy Statement

A statement of educational philosophy is a concise summary (usually about one page) of the portfolio developer's beliefs about teaching and learning. It should provide insight into what kind of teacher the developer is (or will be) and should allow reviewers to judge the consistency of the portfolio evidence as it relates to the philosophy. The philosophy statement typically includes information about the portfolio developer's reasons for entering the field of education, and feelings about teaching and learning, which form the foundation for instructional decisions and for interactions with students, parents, and colleagues.

Developing a broad statement about educational philosophy is a challenging, but very important activity. Below is some guidance to aid in that process:

Step 1
The developer should consider his or her best lessons and identify the common elements related to the design of these lessons. This should help in developing an understanding of the developer's basic *values and beliefs about instruction*.

Step 2

Next, the developer should think about what he or she did to make those lessons successful. This will help develop a sense of the particular ***instructional and classroom management strategies*** that contributed to students' success.

Step 3

Finally, the developer should construct the philosophy statement, which includes core beliefs, and elucidation of the rationale for and sources of these beliefs. Some examples follow.

Core Belief Statement. The portfolio developer might begin with a statement such as:

I believe students learn best when…

I believe it is the role of the teacher to…

I believe a classroom should be a place of …

An example of a completed statement is:

*"**I believe students learn best when** they are actively engaged in learning experiences that connect them to real-world situations."*

Source of Beliefs. The next step is to determine and explain the fundamental reasons for the core beliefs. This explication typically begins with a phrase similar to:

I believe this because…

An example of a completed statement is:

*"**I believe this because** students who can see a real-world need for mastering a topic are more likely to participate and transfer their knowledge to other situations. This type of learning experience provides students with opportunities to engage in critical thinking and problem solving, which will assist in their construction of knowledge and the transfer and application of that knowledge in other settings in school and the world at large."*

Beliefs in Action. The final step is to add evidence that the beliefs have been put into action in providing instruction to students. This involves broadly describing the decisions made and strategies used by the teacher. This explanation often begins with a phrase such as:

This is evidenced in…

I have shown this through…

An example of a completed statement is:

*"**This is evidenced in** my teaching by the fact that I create lessons that revolve around topics that middle school students are very interested in, and I try to establish a classroom structure that involves each student and allows them to contribute to the class discussions. I try to make lessons relate to current events or everyday happenings in my students' lives by learning about their background, their neighborhood and culture."*

Professional Development Plan. The professional development plan provides the reviewer with an understanding of the short- and long-term professional goals of the portfolio developer, as well as current thinking about how those goals can best be achieved. Ideally, this plan will also demonstrate the developer's commitment to lifelong learning. The following elements should be included in the professional development plan:

- **Short-term goals** (those that can reasonably be achieved within two years).

- **Long-term goals** (primarily those that are achievable within five years, but also those that may be accomplished over the career span).

- **A systematic and specific plan** for working toward, monitoring progress on, and achieving short-term goals. (In developing this, all options should be considered, including reading, taking courses, observing master educators, and seeking a mentor.)

- **A general approach** to achieving longer term goals.

- **Any anticipated challenges** that may interfere with goal accomplishment, along with some strategies that may help to overcome them.

Continuing the Portfolio Process

The first attempt at creating a teaching portfolio with the JHU Digital Portfolio will not only allow for the creation of a product, but will guide the developer through the process of reflecting on practice. After mastering these skills, it is likely that an educator will be able to use some artifacts from the initial portfolio, but will modify and restructure it for another purpose or to address a different set of standards or goals. Portfolio development is a powerful professional development tool, one that can assist in tracking progress and demonstrating knowledge and skills to others.

 Discussion Questions

1. Why is it important to include a variety of types of artifacts in your portfolio?

2. Name an example of each type of artifact: validation, reflection, and authentic. Why is it important to include examples of each type in your portfolio?

3. How will you use the portfolio you are developing? How does the purpose change the way you should think about the portfolio content?

4. Why is a clear understanding of the standard critical to the selection of the appropriate artifact?

References for Part I

Arrington & Field (2001) based on the work of: Rodriguez & Sjostrom (1998); McNergney & Herbert (1997); Ross (1987); Schön (1987); Zeichner (1983); Cruickshank (1981); Van Manen (1977); Kolb (1984).

Baratz-Snowden, J. (1995, April). Towards a coherent vision of teacher development. Paper presented at the annual meeting of the American Educational Research Association, San Francisco.

Brubacher, J.W., Case, C.W., & Reagan, T.G. (1994). *Becoming a reflective educator: How to build a culture of inquiry in the schools.* Thousand Oaks, CA: Corwin Press.

Bullough, R.V. & Gitlin, A. (1995) *Becoming a Student of Teaching: Methodologies for Exploring Self and School Context.* New York: Garland

Clarke, J. A. (1995). Tertiary students' perceptions of their learning environments: A new procedure and some outcomes. *Higher Education Research and Development,* 14(1), 1–12.

Cranton, P. (1996). *Professional development as transformative learning: New perspectives for teachers of adults.* San Francisco: Jossey-Bass.

Doolittle, P. (1994). Teacher portfolio assessment. ERIC/AE Digest.

Edgerton, R., Hutchings, P., & Quinlan, K. (1991). The teaching portfolio: Capturing scholarship in teaching. Washington, DC: AAHE.

Fosnot, C.T. (1989). *Enquiring teachers, enquiring learners: A constructivist approach for teaching.* New York: Teachers College Press.

Garmston, R.J. (2001). I know I can. *Journal of Staff Development,* 22(1), 72–73.

Lankard, B.A. (1996). Acquiring self-knowledge for career development. ERIC Digest no. 175.

Liston, D.P., & Zeichner, K.M. (1991). *Teacher education and the social conditions of schooling.* New York: Routledge.

Martin-Kneip, G. (1999) Capturing the wisdom of practice. Retrieved April 2002 from http://www.ascd.org/readingroom/books/martin99.html#ch1

Marzano, R. (1992). *A different kind of classroom.* Alexandria, VA: Association for Supervision and Curriculum Development.

Rodriquez, Y. & Sjostrom, B. (1998). Critical reflection for professional development: A comparative study of nontraditional adult and traditional student teachers. *Journal of Teacher Education,* 49, 177–186.

Stein, D. (2000). Teaching critical reflection: Myths and realities No. 7, ERIC Document.

Valli, L. (Ed.). (1992). *Reflective teacher education: Cases and critiques*. Albany, NY: State University of New York Press.

To learn more about the following organizations, please refer to the contact information below.

NBPTS (National Board for Professional Teaching Standards)
http://www.nbpts.org
National Office
1525 Wilson Blvd, Suite 500
Arlington, VA 22209
703-465-2700

ISTE (International Society for Technology in Education)
http://www.iste.org
Washington, DC Office
1710 Rhode Island Ave NW, Suite 900
Washington, DC 20036
800-654-4777 (U.S. & Canada)
202-861-7777 (International)
202-861-0888 (fax)

CSSCO/INTASC (Council of Chief State School Officers/Interstate New Teacher Assessment and Support Consortium)
http://www.ccsso.org
One Massachusetts Avenue, NW, Suite 700
Washington, DC 20001-1431
voice: 202-336-7000 · fax: 202-408-8072

Adobe Systems, Inc.
http://www.adobe.com
Corporate headquarters
345 Park Avenue
San Jose, CA 95110-2704
Tel: 408-536-6000
Fax: 408-537-6000

Microsoft Corporation
http://www.microsoft.com
Corporate Headquarters
One Microsoft Way
Redmond, WA 98052-6399
425-882-8080
fax 425-936-7329

Part II

Developing Your Own Teaching Portfolio

Chapter 4

Overview and Features of the JHU Digital Portfolio System

The JHU Digital Portfolio is a Web-based portfolio application that provides a repository for evidence of your work from which you can select representative materials to reflect upon and relate to multiple sets of standards. It then allows you to create multiple standards-based portfolios that you can share with others through the creation of Web pages or export to another format for distribution. The JHU Digital Portfolio is designed to be easy to use and support the development of high-quality portfolios by pre-service and in-service teachers as well as other professional educators.

Intuitive and User-friendly

The JHU Digital Portfolio has a simple and straightforward user interface and navigational structure. The main menu is found on the upper left-hand side of each page and is the primary means of navigating through the application to the Home Page, Portfolio, Presentations, Messages, and Tools areas. In addition, at the top of every page in the Portfolio section there is a "breadcrumb trail" that shows where the user is in the application and provides an alternate means of navigating.

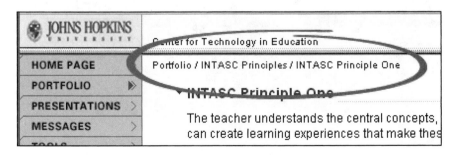

Figure 4.1 "Breadcrumb" Trail

Adaptable to Varied Sets of Standards

The Johns Hopkins University Digital Portfolio was originally built around the INTASC principles, and these are the default standards that organize the Portfolio section where artifacts and reflections are placed. This system also allows users to create their own portfolio structure by adding a new set of standards or goals, such as course, state, or national standards. This feature makes the JHU Digital Portfolio highly useful across the career span and in a wide range of settings.

Facilitates Collaboration and Review

The JHU Digital Portfolio system facilitates collaboration and ongoing review throughout the portfolio's development. The system provides an easy, safe, and secure method for sharing sections of the portfolio with peers, advisors, and members of the portfolio review team. An embedded Message feature allows the portfolio developer to request feedback from any member of the collaborative community, which is typically made up of all faculty and students in the program for which the portfolio is required. This ongoing collaboration and feedback contributes to a deeper level of reflection and leads to a higher quality end product.

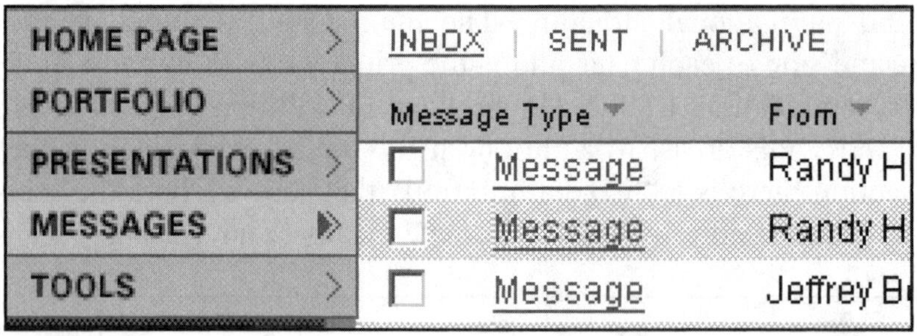

HOME PAGE	>	INBOX	SENT	ARCHIVE	
PORTFOLIO	>	Message Type ▾		From ▾	
PRESENTATIONS	>	☐	Message	Randy H
MESSAGES	▸	☐	Message	Randy H
TOOLS	>	☐	Message	Jeffrey B

Figure 4.2 Message Feature

Two Interfaces for Portfolio Presentation

The JHU Digital Portfolio includes two interfaces of the teaching portfolio.

Working Portfolio

This is a password-protected work-in-progress portfolio. You can easily edit and/or add content to this dynamic working portfolio, as well as keep it up to date with the feedback from peers and advisors.

Presentation Portfolio

This is a public presentation of your work, which the portfolio developer creates and is not editable. This "showcase" version is not password-protected and therefore is available for anyone to view, including reviewers and potential employers who know the unique URL. While this published view of the portfolio is not password-protected, viewers must be provided with the Web address by the portfolio developer. It cannot be found through the simple query of a search engine.

Using the JHU Digital Portfolio, the portfolio developer can create multiple presentations tailored to the specific needs of particular audiences. The presentation created for the academic portfolio review team is typically quite comprehensive; however, a second presentation designed for use during a job search might have a more specific purpose and only include elements of the "master" portfolio. The JHU Digital Portfolio system makes it extremely easy for the user to create multiple presentations and it generates a unique URL for each one.

Portfolio Development Tools

The JHU Digital Portfolio system includes a number of tools to help create high-quality portfolios. The Message Center, which provides a mechanism for ongoing communication about the developing portfolio, and the Presentation publication feature have already been mentioned. In addition, the JHU Digital Portfolio has a Journal tool, which allows the portfolio developer to create narrative reflections within the portfolio environment, and a File Cabinet, which allows users to upload and organize all files that may be included in the portfolio. This File Cabinet tool provides secure storage of files in virtually any format and makes the files readily accessible during the portfolio development process. Finally, both a comprehensive Help feature and integrated tutorial provide directions on how to navigate and use the JHU Digital Portfolio.

Registration and Login

On the inside cover of this guide you will see an access code consisting of six "words." Go to the Web site **http://www.prenhall.com/ jhuportfolio** and enter that access code. Each access code allows you to register one licensed copy of the JHU Digital Portfolio.

After you have logged in, you will be automatically directed to another screen where you can enter your registration information. You will first create your login (username) and password. Your login should be six to twelve alphanumeric characters. Your password should be at least four alphanumeric characters and something you can easily remember. You may change your login and password at any time by accessing the Tools/Setting screen within the portfolio application. If you choose a login already in use, you will then be prompted to select another login.

After creating your login and password, you will be on the last step of the registration process. The underlined fields are required. Keep in mind that you may change this information at any time by logging into the portfolio and clicking on Tools then Settings.

On the personal information screen, you will be prompted to add a picture of yourself. It will be a part of both your working portfolio as well as your presentation portfolio. Your picture should be approximately 120 x 150 pixels in size. Check the Help box if you need help adjusting the size. If you do not have a suitable picture at hand, leave the picture field blank and add one later. You may also insert an avatar (computer-generated character image), a school logo, or other image. Keep in mind that the image you choose will be visible through your presentation portfolio and should be of a professional nature.

The Five Domains of the Digital Portfolio

Now you are ready to begin developing your digital portfolio. Here is a brief overview of the five major portfolio sections, which will be covered in much greater detail later in this chapter.

The five domains of the JHU Digital Portfolio are:

- **Home Page,** which includes the *Introduction, Educational Philosophy,* and *Professional Development Plan.*

- **Portfolio,** which is the working portfolio, where artifacts are aligned with standards, written interpretations of those standards are recorded, and artifact rationales are found with the all-important supporting evidence (the artifact itself).

- **Messages,** which is where you can send and receive messages and keep track of ongoing and archived correspondence.

- **Tools,** which contains the File Cabinet (where all documents and support files are stored), the Journal (a private online space for creating and storing journal entries), the Settings area (where the user profile can be updated), and the Directory (where you can set up groups within your digital portfolio community and send group e-mails).

- **Presentation,** which is where you select individual elements for a presentation portfolio and publish it.

Navigate among these five domain areas by clicking one of the shaded titles on the upper left side of your screen. If you want to move quickly to a specific section of your portfolio, float your mouse over the domain titles to see the list of contents for each domain. (**Note:** If there is no content in that domain, nothing will appear to the right of the title.)

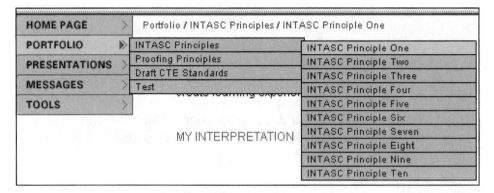

Figure 4.3 The Five Domain Areas

Home Page

Once you have logged into your portfolio and arrive at the home page, you will see the domain navigation (home page, portfolio, presentation, messages, and tools) on the left side of your screen with some additional elements on the upper right (feedback, help, contact, and logout). These areas will remain visible as you move through the portfolio. There are also several blank text areas on the home page titled *Introduction*, *Educational Philosophy*, and *Professional Development Plan*. Also referred to as the framework section of your portfolio, this framework section is where you set the context of your portfolio for yourself and for reviewers. We discuss in this guide some recommended content for these sections, but please contact your instructor or advisor for specific content requirements.

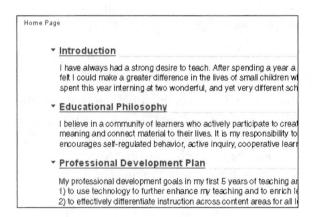

Figure 4.4 *Introduction, Educational Philosophy,* and *Professional Development Plan* Home Page

The *Introduction* provides viewers of your portfolio with background information about you, your teaching experiences (formal and informal), and other details that you would like to share.

The *Educational Philosophy* section contains information about your educational values—what you think about teaching and learning, and why you were drawn to education as a career. It represents to the world your views about the educational process. These views are the foundation for the educational and instructional decisions you make (or will make) every day in the classroom and in your interactions with students, colleagues, and other educational stakeholders. Your philosophy of education, therefore, should be a concise accounting of your beliefs about teaching and learning and should be consistent with the contents displayed in your portfolio.

Since your education does not end when you graduate or complete your program, the *Professional Development Plan* section is provided as a location to describe your education and career goals. Your professional development plan should outline your goals as well as a systematic plan for meeting those goals. This plan could include taking courses, reading literature, or finding a mentor. Articulating your career goals is your first step toward accomplishing them.

You will notice as we move through the portfolio that each area of the application functions in much the same way. As you become familiar with the navigation of the application on the home page, the rest of your portfolio development will just fall into place.

Adding Content

The three areas of content on the home page *(Introduction, Educational Philosophy,* and *Professional Development)* all have an Edit and Close button opposite them on the right side of the screen. Enter content by clicking on the Edit button. The top of the screen opens to an area where you enter and, later, edit your text. You can compose directly into this editing box, or preferably, cut and paste your text from a word-processing application. If you choose to cut and paste text from a word-processing application, please note that some formatting may disappear and will have to be added using HTML tags.

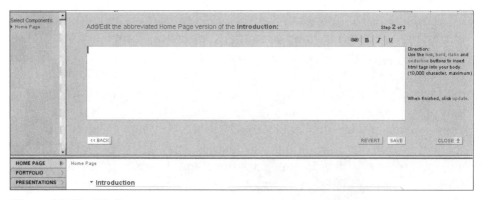

Figure 4.5 The Edit Screen

Quick Clicks: Text Entering/Editing Screen

1. **Save** will record the content you added. You must click **Save** to keep the text you entered.

2. **Back** returns you to the home page without saving any changes you have made.

3. **Revert** deletes all changes since the last time you saved (updated) your content.

4. **Close** returns you to the home page without saving any changes you have made.

Because the JHU Digital Portfolio is a Web-based application, all content that you enter must be configured to display as a Web page. HTML tags dictate how your content will appear on the Web site. Therefore, you will need to use HTML tags to create links to external Web sites and as well as to format text. It is not necessary for you to learn HTML (hyper-text markup language) to format your text. Use the buttons above the right part of the text box (B = bold, I = italic and U = underline) to format your text with the appropriate HTML tags. In the text box, you will see the appropriate HTML tags displayed around the selected text, and, below the text box, you will see the properly formatted text as it will be displayed on the Web. This process is the same whether you are entering content on your home page or in other parts of your portfolio.

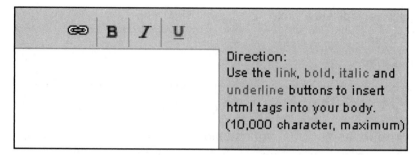

Figure 4.6 HTML Tag Formatting Screen

Quick Clicks: Framework

Follow these steps to add text:

1. Click the **Edit** button to the right of *Introduction, Educational Philosophy,* or *Professional Development.*

2. The screen is split in two with the following at the top of your window. Notice the arrow at left pointing to the section where you are working, as well as the text near the top that says "Edit the complete Introduction." These are to help orient you as you begin working.

3. The bottom half of your screen is below.

4. Enter your text in the box using the bold, italic, and underline formatting buttons, if necessary.

5. Click **Save** to save your text. You then see how your text appears in your portfolio in the bottom half of your screen.

6. Close your text box.

How do I edit text?

Editing text is similar to adding it.

1. Click **Edit.** This brings you back to the split screen with text box at the top. You can then do any of the following.

2. Make changes, additions or deletions to existing text. (Revert will return your text to the last saved version.) Add links and HTML tags. (See pages 52, 54–56 for information.)

3. Be sure to click **Save.**

4. Click **Close** to save your changes.

How do I delete text?

1. Click **Edit.**

2. Highlight and delete all text.

3. Click **Save.**

4. Click **Close.**

This portfolio application will support HTML codes, if you are fortunate enough to have some Web development skills. Please remember, however, that the real focus and purpose of your portfolio is on the content and reflections that you include, not on the color of the font. Although there are a number of ways to customize digital portfolio content, including using HTML tags, we strongly recommended that you spend the majority of your time perfecting interpretations and rationales rather than adding complex and often distracting graphics to your portfolio. In most cases, portfolio assessment is contingent on quality of content, not elaborate design elements.

That said, the JHU Digital Portfolio does provide members with a quick and easy way to bold, italicize, and underline text as well as include links to other Web sites. Once you choose to add or edit content, you will be taken to an editable text area. Above the text box there are four icons: link, bold, italicize, and underline.

Quick Clicks: Adding HTML Tags

Follow these steps to add the appropriate formatting (HTML) tags:

1. Use your mouse to highlight the content you would like to modify.

2. Click the appropriate icon—bold, italicize, or underline.

3. HTML tags will be added just before and just after the text you highlighted.

4. Click **Save** and then **Close.**

You can also link to an existing Web page or a file located in your File Cabinet, such as your résumé. You might wish to present a Web page you constructed during your student teaching experience or simply showcase your Web development skills.

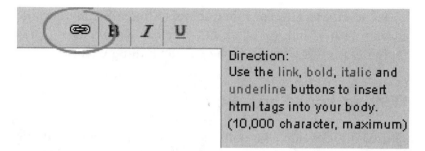

Figure 4.7 Linking to an Existing Web Page

Quick Clicks: Adding a Link and Linking to a Web Page

Linking text to a specific URL works in much the same way:

1. In the Edit screen, place your cursor where you would like to insert the link text.
2. Type in the text you would like to be an active link.
3. Highlight the text you would like to be an active link.
4. Click the **Link** icon just to the left of the Bold icon.
5. A small window will appear on the screen, containing the words you highlighted to be used for this link.
6. Click **OK.**
7. A window will appear on the screen, click on Web Link.
8. Enter the URL of the page you would like to link to (example: http://www.yahoo.com).
9. Click **OK** again.
10. Click **Save** and then **Close.**

Adding a Link to Your Portfolio

From the Edit screen, simply place your cursor where you would like to enter the link. Type in the text you would like to be an active link. Highlight that text and click on the link symbol. A small window appears displaying the label to be used for this link. The label is the actual text that appears in your portfolio as an active link. After you click OK, select Web Link to enter a URL or File Cabinet to find a file in your File Cabinet that you wish to link to. Click OK to close that window. Then click Save before you click Close, which exits the Editing window.

Using HTML in Your Portfolio

You will not need it to develop your portfolio, but you might enjoy learning a little about Web page development and HTML code. There are literally hundreds of Web sites devoted to the HTML amateur and professional.

Here are a few sites we recommend that will provide you with a good overview of the process, color charts, and design tips:

http://hotwired.lycos.com/webmonkey/reference/html_cheatsheet/
http://www.psacake.com/web/dy.asp
http://www.alphalink.com.au/~rhduncan/htmlguide/cheatindex.html

If you prefer, learn more about HTML and writing for the Web through courses offered in your area at community centers or at your local community college.

Request Feedback

After you have text entered into any of the areas on your home page (and in other areas throughout your portfolio), you will see a new button visible to the right of the text called Req. Feedback. This is the button you click to ask another member of your portfolio community for feedback (i.e., critical commentary) on your content. This feature allows you to easily maintain a running conversation over weeks or months about elements of your portfolio with other members of the portfolio community. This button is only visible when you have added content.

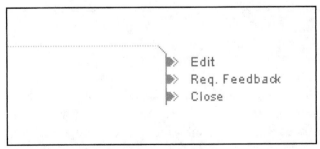

Figure 4.8 Request Feedback Feature

We will talk more about the Feedback feature and the Message Center later in the guide.

Tools: File Cabinet

Now that you are familiar with the home page or framework section, we will move on to the Tools. The Tools area provides JHU Digital Portfolio members with access to the File Cabinet, Journal, Settings, and Directory areas of the application. The File Cabinet gives members the ability to upload and organize files, folders, and links that may eventually be added to the Portfolio area. There is a maximum of 100 megabytes (MB) of storage space allowed for your portfolio files. As a note, the average portfolio generally runs less than 20 MB. When you approach the limit of storage, you will receive a message letting you know that you should delete or compress some files before uploading new files.

The File Cabinet

This is where you upload, store, and organize your files and documents. Before a file, video, document, or Web site can be added to your portfolio, it must first be added to your File Cabinet. Technically, when you add documents to your working portfolio, you are merely linking to files already stored in your File Cabinet. Files must be in your File Cabinet to be included in your portfolio.

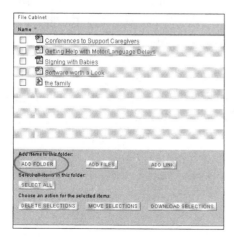

Figure 4.9 Add Folder Feature

Quick Clicks: Adding a Folder to the File Cabinet

To add a folder to the File Cabinet:

1. From the home page, click **Tools** on the main menu.

2. From the Tools main page, click **File Cabinet.**

3. You will be taken automatically to the File Cabinet.

4. If you want to add a sub-folder to an existing folder, navigate to that folder and then click on the folder icon (or name). Otherwise, remain on the main File Cabinet page.

5. Click **Add Folder.** A small box will appear on the screen.

6. Put your cursor in the **Name** field, and type a name for the folder you are adding. (Remember to use a name that will be easily recognizable later.)

7. Put your cursor in the **Description** field, and type a description for the new folder.

8. Click **Add.**

9. The new folder is now available in your File Cabinet.

While any type of digital media may be stored in your File Cabinet, organization is the key. You will collect dozens, if not hundreds, of documents over the course of your academic program or throughout the construction of your portfolio, and being able to locate those files months or years later is vitally important. So as you collect your documents for inclusion in your portfolio, name them appropriately so you will be able to easily locate them.

In addition to deliberately naming files, use the folder structure to organize the location of those files. In the Digital Portfolio, you may create folders within folders just as on your computer.

The Way It Works

Files appearing in your working portfolio and, subsequently, in your presentation portfolio are actually links to files in your File Cabinet. They have not been moved or copied from the File Cabinet to the portfolio. Therefore, if files are deleted from your File Cabinet, they will no longer be accessible from your working portfolio or any resulting portfolio presentation you have created.

When you view the File Cabinet page, you will notice several buttons at the bottom of the page: Add Folder, Add Files, and Add Link. Initially, the top part of the page will be empty; this is where you will view your files after you have uploaded them. Start out by creating several folders to hold your files. As your portfolio grows, you may need to add sub-folders—this is done the same way.

Click on the Add Folder button. You will then see a new window with a text line to name your new folder and a space for a description of the contents of that folder. Once you have completed those two areas, click on Add. The window will close automatically.

You can add as many folders as you like, and files can be moved around between folders as you organize your materials. You will have an opportunity to not only name your file, but to also write a description for each file you upload to the File Cabinet. The description is visible when you click on the icon next to the document name in the File Cabinet. Your description could include the name of your document, when you created it, for what purpose, when it was used, and the result. The more information you can record about each file you upload, the easier it will be to identify specific files months later.

In addition to adding files and folders to your File Cabinet, you can also add links to live Web pages that you created yourself, or that are related to your portfolio in some way. For instance, you may wish to link to the Web site of the school where you completed your internship, or to a Web site you created for another course you are taking. Just remember, if you think you might want to include an item in your portfolio, it must first be added to your File Cabinet!

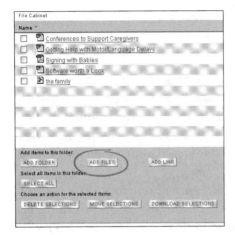

Figure 4.10 Add Files Feature

Quick Clicks: Adding Files

To add a file to the File Cabinet:

1. From the home page, click **Tools** on the main menu.
2. From the Tools main page, click **File Cabinet.**
3. You will automatically be taken to the File Cabinet.

If you want to add the file to a particular folder, navigate to that folder and then click on the highlighted folder name. You are now ready to add the file:

1. Click **Add Files.**
2. A gray box will appear on the screen.
3. Put your cursor in the **Name** field, and type a name for the file you're adding (remember to use a name that will be easily recognizable later).
4. Click **Browse**, locate the file you want to attach and then click **Open.** The dialog box will close and the file path will be visible in the Browse text box.
5. Put your cursor in the **Description** field, and type a description for the new file.
6. Add the file type, if known. The system will recognize most file types form their name extension.
7. Click **Add.**

The new file is now available in your File Cabinet.

To add a file to your File Cabinet, the file can be stored on portable media, your computer's hard drive or be a link from the Web. In addition to folders and files (which may consist of documents, images, video and audio files) you can also add Web sites to your File Cabinet through the Add Link feature.

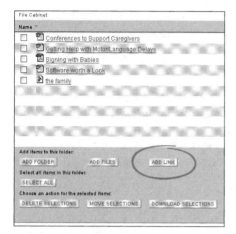

Figure 4.11   Add Link Feature

Quick Clicks: Adding a Link

To add a link to your File Cabinet:

1. From the home page, click **Tools** on the main menu.

2. From the Tools main page, click **File Cabinet.**

3. You will be taken automatically to the File Cabinet.

If you want to add the link to a particular folder, navigate to that folder and then click on the highlighted folder name.

You are now ready to add the link:

1. Click **Add Link.**

2. A gray box will appear on the screen.

3. Put your cursor in the **Name** field, and type a name for the file you're adding. (Remember to use a name that will be easily recognizable later.)

4. Put your cursor in the **URL** field, and type the URL of the link you're adding.

5. Put your cursor in the **Description** field, and type a description for the link.

6. Click **Add.**

The link is now available in your File Cabinet and from here can be added to your working portfolio.

Viewing Files

Now that you have added folders, files, and links to your File Cabinet, you may wonder, "So how do I look at them?" To view the items in your File Cabinet, click on the title of the file. To view the description, click on the icon next to the file title.

Uploading and Downloading Files

Please remember that the files in your portfolio's File Cabinet are stored on servers accessible through the Internet. During the time files are transferred from that remote location to your computer, you may experience a delay that will vary based on the speed of your connection to the Internet as well as the size of the file. While your File Cabinet can hold files up to a total of 100 MB in size, it is important to think about the size of documents and files before your upload them to your file cabinet. Whatever goes into your portfolio (uploaded) must come out (downloaded) in order to be viewed. So please consider the conditions under which your reviewers, faculty members, peers, and other viewers of your portfolio will be connecting to the Internet. This is especially important when working with images and video. When you are working with video files, consider whether a 30-second video will convey the essentially the same message as a two-minute video. Consider the size of the pictures you want to upload to your File Cabinet, and make them no larger than necessary. This is not to discourage you from using video and images files in your portfolio, but rather to encourage you to think about your viewer and the ease of both downloading and uploading.

Video and audio files are not the only file types that merit your attention. Since whatever you put into the JHU Digital Portfolio must be able to be viewed by yourself and others from any Internet-connected computer, it is important to use the most universal file formats available in order to minimize any viewing or downloading problems. Although the JHU Digital Portfolio can support any file format that you can transmit on the Web, it is essential to remember that unless your target audience can view the file, its inclusion in your portfolio is useless. Our recommendations noted here are strictly to help you select the file formats for your uploaded files and should be taken as guidelines, not absolutes.

If you are working through a telephone modem, often referred to as "dial-up," your delay will be greater than someone accessing the Internet through a broadband connection, DSL, or a cable modem. Obviously, the larger the file, the longer it will take to transfer.

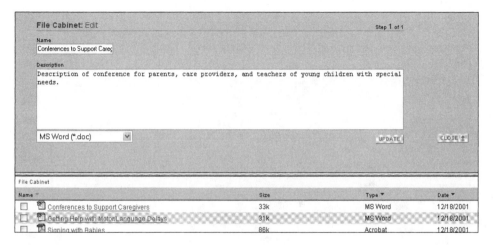

Figure 4.12 Edit Feature

Quick Clicks: Renaming Files

1. From the home page, click **Tools** on the main menu.

2. From the Tools main page, click **File Cabinet.**

3. You will automatically be taken to the File Cabinet.

4. To view a file/link, click on the **File Name** to open the document.

5. The link or file will open in a new window.

6. Clicking on the Icon will allow you to rename the file and/or change the description and file type.

Moving Files/Folders

As you continue collecting documents and other artifacts for your portfolio, you may wish to reorganize your File Cabinet by moving the files from one folder to another and creating folders within folders (sub-folders). This is easy to accomplish by using the Move Selections button at the bottom of the File Cabinet screen.

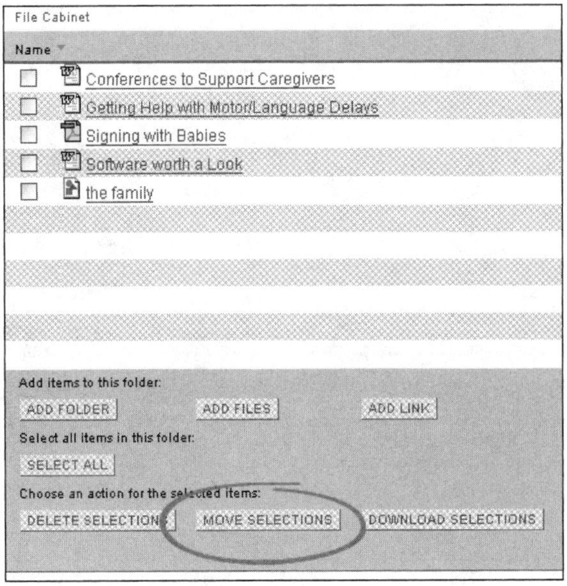

Figure 4.13 Move Selections Feature

After reviewing your folders and files and determining which you would like to move and where, click the check box next to the file(s) you wish to move into another folder. A small box will appear on the screen. Simply check which folder you would like the files to be moved into and click OK. You have just moved your files! Follow the same process to create sub-folders within a master folder.

Perhaps you wish to organize your files by course or semester. You can create course folders and then at the end of the semester, move all the course folders into the appropriate semester folder. You may move files and folders around as much as you wish; nothing about the file, its name, or the description you wrote will change, just simply its location.

Quick Clicks: Moving Selections Within the File Cabinet

It is possible to move files, folders, and links within the File Cabinet:

1. From the home page, click **Tools** on the main menu.
2. From the Tools main page, click **File Cabinet.**
3. You will automatically be taken to the File Cabinet.
4. Use the check box next to each message to select the file, link or folder to move.
5. Click **Move Selections.**
6. A small box will appear on the screen.
7. Click on the folder into which you'd like to move the selected file, folder, or links.
8. Click **Move File(s).**

The selected files, folders, and links are now available in their new location.

Deleting Files

In addition to moving items around in your File Cabinet, you can also delete files and folders that are no longer necessary. Be very careful about deleting files and folders from your File Cabinet. Files and folders are deleted the same way. Select the files and/or folders that you wish to delete and click in the check box next to each item.

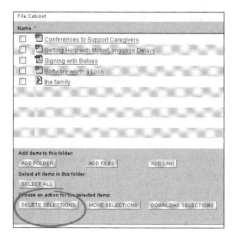

Figure 4.14 Delete Selections Feature

At the bottom of the File Cabinet screen is the Delete Selections button. After you have selected all items you wish to delete, click on the Delete Selections button. You will get a warning message on the screen informing you that this action is permanent and cannot be undone. You may click OK to continue the operation, or Cancel to stop it.

Please be careful. Once an item—file or folder—has been deleted, it cannot be retrieved.

Selecting All Files

By following the buttons on the bottom of the File Cabinet screen, you can select all files, delete selected files, move selected files, or download selected files.

Quick Clicks: Selecting All Files

To select all files in the File Cabinet (in order to delete or for another purpose):

1. From the home page, click **Tools** on the main menu.

2. From the Tools main page, click **File Cabinet.**

3. You will be taken automatically to the File Cabinet.

4. Click **Select All.**

5. The check box to the left of each file, folder, or link on the page will be checked.

6. If you would like to delete all of the selected files, folder, and links, click **Delete Selections.** Please note, however, that the delete function is permanent. It cannot be undone.

Downloading Files

The download feature allows you to save the file, or selected files, to the hard drive of your computer, or other media storage device (see Figure 4.15 on page 67). When you download a file from your portfolio File Cabinet, it does not delete that file. The file is still available in your File Cabinet.

Depending on the file size you are downloading, it may take quite a while to transfer the file or files to your computer. A new window will open which will tell you which files you are downloading how large they are and how long it will take to download them.

The files will be saved to the default download file on your computer. In most cases, in order to download files as efficiently as possible, the files will be automatically zipped, or compressed. These files may easily be uncompressed (restored to their original size) by using the free WINZIP utility. (Go to **www.winzip.com** or **www.download.com** for more information.)

Figure 4.15 Download Selections Feature

File Types

It may be helpful to think of the JHU Digital Portfolio as a two-way process. Whatever you upload to the File Cabinet (and then linked into your portfolio) must be "downloaded" to be viewed by your instructor or reviewers. In most cases, the reviewer must have the specific software loaded on his machine in order to view files you have uploaded. In order to avoid file incompatibility, we have determined some suggested formats and file types. Please consider these file formats as suggestions, not absolutes.

There are several different categories of files: text files, image files, audio files, and video files. The following paragraphs will provide you with suggestions for using text and image files. Some programs are almost a universal standard due to their widespread use and dominance in the marketplace. Microsoft Office Suite products, including Word and

Excel, are two universal standards. Although these may be prevalent in your computer lab, many home computers come pre-loaded with the MS Works package, not the MS Office Suite. Please keep in mind there are substantial differences in these products, and although files created in MS Works and MS Word have great similarities, the files are not universally interchangeable.

Text Files

If you have access to the Adobe Acrobat software, we encourage you to save your files as Portable Document Format (PDF) files before uploading them to your File Cabinet. The Acrobat format essentially makes documents "read-only" while maintaining existing formatting. Additionally, Adobe Acrobat is the industry standard for the exchange of electronic files across different computers and platforms. A free "Acrobat Reader" is available for use when viewing these files.

Files named with the PDF extension are in the Portable Document Format. Files in this format retain consistent formatting and layout even when exchanged across different computer platforms. As a universal file format, PDF files retain all of the fonts, formatting, colors, and graphics of any source document, regardless of the application and platform used to create it. This format solves commonly encountered problems in electronic document distribution, such as allowing you to read documents that were created with software you may not have yourself, and gives you the ability to display and in many cases print these documents exactly as they were created. Another advantage is that PDF files are usually much smaller than the original file (e.g., a PDF version of a Word file containing many graphs and figures could be four times smaller, without any loss of content). These features together make .pdf a recommended file format for use in your electronic portfolio.

If you do not have access to Adobe Acrobat, our second suggestion is to use Rich Text Format (RTF). RTF was developed by Microsoft Corporation. Although it does not store enough layout information about a document to ensure WYSIWYG (What You See is What You Get) platform portability, most word processors support the RTF format. It is important to remember that any documents containing graphics prior to being converted to (saved as) RTF and then re-opened as an RTF document may not contain the original document graphics. Additionally, RTF may not maintain your original formatting.

Image Files

An image file in your portfolio can communicate much more than text alone. Whether it is a digital photo of your students' work, a scanned photo of yourself teaching, a short video of you working with a small group of students, or something else, including photographs, videos, and other graphic images can greatly enhance your portfolio.

To make the make the most of your work, make sure that the images, videos, and audio files you include demonstrate the feature, skill, or lesson you intend. Remember that although a picture is worth a thousand words, the right picture/image is priceless.

While video and pictures can be a valuable addition to your portfolio, please consider the following questions before uploading your photo album to the File Cabinet:

1. Does use of the image file increase comprehension or the demonstration of concepts?
2. How will others be accessing the image, through a modem connection or via broadband? (Remember, everything uploaded must get downloaded. The larger the picture, the larger the file size. Larger files take longer to upload and download and may not be worth the difference.)
3. How important is the image quality of the material?
4. Do you have permission to use the images? (See Figure 4.16 on page 72 for sample photo release forms.)
5. Is the image file a more effective or efficient means of communicating the information, or is it just replacing another effective method?

After you have considered these questions and have decided to include graphic images in your portfolios, it is time to learn a little about the various formats and their effectiveness on the Web.

There are two elements that contribute to the file size—size and resolution. The larger the size of the image, (as measured by the number of pixels), the more space the image file occupies. For this reason, some cameras allow you to specify the file size when you take a picture. Although you are likely to get better results with a higher resolution image, it isn't always needed, especially when the image is going to be displayed on the Web or printed very small. In these cases smaller images (and lower resolution) will suffice. Because each image will have a smaller file size, you'll be able to hold more images in the camera's memory. Take some time to learn how to use your digital camera as well as the scanner. This can save you the several extra steps involved in compressing a file or saving it to a .jpg (JPEG) format.

We recommend the .jpg file format for use with the JHU Digital Portfolio. The .jpg format compresses image files to a very small file size—often by as much as 90% or to only 1/10 of the size of the original, which is very good when they are to be used for Web sites and e-mail. This is especially important if your portfolio will be accessed through a modem (as opposed to a broadband connection). Although there are several other file formats which are quite suitable including .bmp (bitmap) and .tif (TIFF), the .jpg format is the recommended file format to use when saving photographs and other images for inclusion in your portfolio.

Using Video

Think about it… How better to demonstrate your ability to teach a lesson in your class, than to include a video of you doing so? Video is a wonderful tool for teachers! Video is so effective that many teacher education programs actually require students/interns to videotape themselves delivering a lesson. Today's video cameras are so small that they can be quite unnoticeable in a classroom. But before you set up your tripod and press record on your camera, think about why you want to use video in your electronic portfolio. Think about the specific events you wish to capture and how to best do that. In addition to the content of your video clip, think about the length of the video clip you want to include.

As a Web-based application, the JHU Digital Portfolio has some limitations. We've provided some recommendations that will make including video in your portfolio effective and efficient. As you consider video, ask yourself the following questions:

1. Does use of the video enhance a viewer's comprehension or your demonstration of concepts?

2. How will viewers be accessing the video? Through a modem connection or via broadband? (Remember, everything uploaded must get downloaded.)

3. What type of video will you be using ("talking head," demonstration of a detailed procedure, an animation, a series of stills with audio)?

4. Do you have permission to use the video clips you have chosen? It is essential to have permission from parents or legal guardians when including images on students. And as a safeguard, never include any identifying information along with the student images, such as full name, age, etc. (See Figure 4.16 on page 72 for sample photo release forms.)

5. And most important, is video the best way to demonstrate your competency, or is it just replacing another effective method?

After you have considered these questions, and have decided that video is the right medium to demonstrate a particular skill or competency, there are four additional factors to consider: picture size, frame rate, compression, and quality.

When you are using a digital video camera, you may be able to select the frame rate, or the number of frames per second. The more frames per second, the greater the clarity of your video, and the larger the file size. Because cameras vary greatly, we can only provide some basic guidelines to follow. Practice with your camera and understand how it works before the day of your special event.

Before you pull out the camera, make sure that your video clip will demonstrate the skill or competency that you desire. If you want to video yourself teaching, it is helpful to have someone to run the camera, but if you are on your own, just follow a couple of basic rules:

1. Use a tripod. Most cameras have a screw hole on the bottom where a tripod will attach. Just tighten the screw into the camera and then extend the legs of the tripod to the desired height. This is much easier, as well as safer, than trying to balance your camera on top of a bookcase, filing cabinet or desk.

2. Place the camera at an angle where you will not capture your students' faces. This will help you avoid the extra step of obtaining permission. [However, we strongly suggest that you obtain the appropriate permission from your students or their parents/legal guardian. You can do this at the beginning of the school year and keep the photo release forms (see Figure 4.16 on page 72) on file. While not always feasible, as a courtesy, let your

students' parents/legal guardians know when you will be taking pictures or videos in class.]

3. Wear a microphone (if appropriate). While some higher end cameras have built-in directional microphones, most of the more commonly available models do not. A viewer of your portfolio does not necessarily want to hear the sound of desks and chairs moving and papers rustling in your classroom. If you cannot position the camera near you, then you should wear a microphone.

4. Edit your video down to the crucial elements (less than 90 seconds is appropriate in most cases). Remember these two points. First of all, whatever you upload into your portfolio must be downloaded to be viewed. Please be considerate of those viewers who may be accessing your portfolio from a 56K modem connection. Second, a well-edited video clip of less than 30 seconds can be extremely powerful. One of the biggest mistakes people make with video is including clips that are too long. Video is a very powerful tool; a little goes a long way.

Photo Release Form

Date:_____

I_____,
consent to the use of photos and/or videos taken

of me by_____
        (photographer's name).

I understand that such photographs or videos may be used for inclusion in a professional portfolio. And for educational purposes in various media (i.e. print, video, Internet etc.)

Signature:_____

Address:_____

Work Phone: _____

Home Phone: _____

Photo Release Form for Minors

Date:_____

I consent to the use of photos and/or videos taken of my minor child by

_____
        (photographer's name).

I understand that such photographs or videos may be used for educational purposes in various media (i.e. print, video, Internet etc.), specifically, a professional portfolio.

Name of Child: _____

Name of Parent or Legal Guardian:
_____

Signature of Parent or Legal Guardian:
_____

Relationship to Child: _____
Address: _____
Work Phone: _____
Home Phone:_____

Figure 4.16 Sample Photo Release Forms

TIPS for Video File Formats

The MPEG Format. Our recommended format, the MPEG (Moving Pictures Expert Group) format, is the most popular format on the Internet. Video files captured in the MPEG format have the extension .mpg or .mpeg. The MPEG format is cross-platform, meaning it works on PCs and Apple computers (and some PDAs and other devices) and it is supported by all the most popular Web browsers. These factors make it the video file format of choice for your JHU Digital Portfolio.

QuickTime Format. Developed by Apple Computer, QuickTime is another common format on the Internet. Videos stored in the QuickTime format have the extension .mov. Apple computers read QuickTime automatically. It can be viewed on a Windows computer by installing a free player. Not difficult to do; it's just an extra step for your audience.

Tools—Journal: Your Diary, Record, Log, and Memoir

The Tools section of your portfolio also contains a Journal feature. The Journal provides portfolio community members with an electronic tool for recording personal and professional observations. These can also be added to the portfolio as evidence.

The Journal feature is a great way for you to keep a private log of your thoughts, ideas, opinions, and feelings as you move through your program. It is a private space for recording and storing reflections and thoughts about professional and related experiences. Journal entries are listed chronologically, with the most recent entry listed first.

While Journal entries are private and viewable only by the portfolio owner, the application does allow for conversion of entries to artifacts in order to help demonstrate growth over time. When a Journal entry is added to your File Cabinet, it can then be added to the portfolio. At that point you may ask for feedback on your Journal entry and it may be treated like any other file in your portfolio.

Many programs require, or at the very least recommend, that students maintain a Journal during their internship experiences and/or their induction year. This feature allows you to add these Journal entries into your portfolio if you feel it is appropriate. Many portfolio developers like to emphasize the educational journey they have experienced and, by including Journal entries from the beginning, middle, and end of your program, you can demonstrate this growth over time. When you write a Journal entry it is automatically date-stamped, and you can add an appropriate title to your entry. At any time, you may go in and edit your Journal entry.

Journal entries are especially helpful in writing reflections and the narrative pieces that accompany the supporting evidence in your portfolio. And while it may be difficult to write a daily Journal entry, a weekly recap of your experiences, feelings, successes, and challenges can be especially meaningful.

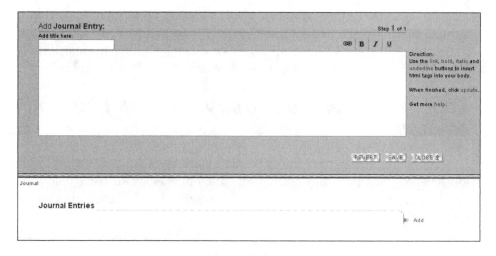

Figure 4.17 Journal Entries Feature

Quick Clicks: Adding a Journal Entry

1. From the home page, click **Tools** on the main menu.
2. From the Tools main page, click **Journal.**
3. Click **Add.**
4. An add/edit box will open on your screen.
5. Place your cursor in the smaller text box, and type a short title for your entry.
6. Place your cursor in the larger text box, and type the content of your journal entry.
7. When you are done, click **Save** and then **Close.**

8. **Revert** deletes all changes since the last time you saved (updated) your content.

9. **Close** returns you to the home page without saving any changes you have made.

Note: See Quick Clicks: Adding HTML Tags on page 54 to include Bold, Italic, and Underlined text.

To edit a Journal entry, not as much for content as for proofreading, open the particular Journal entry you wish to edit, click the Edit button next to the particular Journal entry you wish to edit, and a gray box will open on your screen. Place your cursor in the text box and make any editing changes you feel are necessary. Remember to click Save when you have completed your editing. There is no limit to the number of times you can edit a Journal entry.

Quick Clicks: Editing a Journal Entry

To edit a Journal entry:

1. From the home page, click **Tools** on the main menu.
2. From the Tools main page, click **Journal.**
3. Click **Edit** next to the Journal entry you would like to edit.
4. An edit box will open on your screen.
5. Place the cursor in the text box you would like to edit and make your changes.
6. When you are done, click **Save** and then **Close.**
7. **Revert** deletes all changes since the last time you saved (updated) your content.
8. **Close** returns you to the home page.

Adding a Journal Entry to Your Portfolio

One of the valuable features of the embedded Journal is your ability to add these Journal entries to your portfolio. If you have ever kept a personal journal, you can understand the value in looking back over entries you wrote many months or years before. While you may easily remember events, you may not as easily recall your feelings and viewpoints. As you develop your portfolio over several months or several years, you may find occasions when your Journal entries serve as vital reminders. Often, a Journal entry can illustrate your competency in an area far better than any other type of evidence.

As stated earlier, before an item can become part of your portfolio, you must first add it to your File Cabinet. The first time you add a Journal entry to your File Cabinet, a folder named Journal entries is automatically created. After you have added a Journal entry to your file cabinet, it cannot be edited. You can edit the Journal entry through the Journal page and add it to your File Cabinet again, but the original entry cannot be changed.

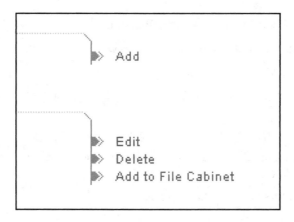

Figure 4.18 Adding a Journal Entry

Quick Clicks: Adding a Journal Entry to the File Cabinet

To add a Journal entry to the File Cabinet:

1. From the home page, click **Tools** on the main menu.
2. From the Tools main page, click **Journal.**
3. Click **Add to File Cabinet** next to the appropriate Journal entry.
4. An edit box will appear on the screen.
5. Put your cursor in the Title field and edit the Journal Title if necessary.
6. Put your cursor in the Description field and type a brief description of the entry. (This will help you find the Journal entry later.)
7. Click **Save.**
8. Your entry will be added to the **Journal Entries** folder in the File Cabinet.

Other Features of Tools: Settings

During your portfolio experience, you may experience life changes, new e-mail, new address, or a new look. The settings section allows you to update your personal information, change your login and password, and upload a new image of yourself. Please remember that all of the personal information that you present in this section of your portfolio will be available to other members in your portfolio community. Keep this in mind when adding an address or other personal contact information. Only your e-mail and first and last name are required.

You can access the Settings section at any time. There is no limit to the number of times you can change your login, password, or other information.

How to Edit Your Username and Password

Your Username and Password are determined during the JHU Digital Portfolio registration process. However, once you start using the application you will have the opportunity to change them. As with most secure applications, we recommend changing your password on a regular basis.

Quick Clicks: Changing Your Password and Username

1. From the home page, click **Tools** on the main menu.
2. From the Tools main page, click **Settings.**
3. You will be taken automatically to the Settings page within the Digital Portfolio.
4. Click **Edit** to the right of the words Login/Password.
5. A gray edit box will appear on the screen.

If you want to change your login:

1. Put your cursor in the box marked New Login and type your new login.
2. Click **Save** and **Close** when you're done.

If you want to change your password:

1. Put your cursor in the box marked Current Password and type your password.
2. Put your cursor in the box marked New Password and type a new password.
3. Put your box in the box marked Confirm New Password and retype your new password.
4. Click **Save** and **Close** when you're done.
5. **Clear** deletes all of the text in the text boxes so that you can start over.

How to Add/Edit Personal Information

Your personal information is added automatically to the application during the JHU Digital Portfolio registration process. One you start using the application, you can make changes.

Quick Clicks: Adding/Editing Your Personal Information

1. From the home page, click **Tools** on the main menu.
2. From the Tools main page, click **Settings.**
3. You will be taken automatically to the Settings page within the Digital Portfolio.

4. Click **Edit** to the right of your Personal Information.

5. A gray edit box will appear on the screen.

6. Put your cursor in each box you want to edit, and make your changes.

7. Click **Save** and **Close** when you're done.

8. Your Personal Information should now be updated.

9. Click **Close** to complete the process.

In many cases, it is helpful to have a photo of you, the portfolio developer, as part of your portfolio. Whether you are developing a portfolio for a course, for an end-of-program assessment, or as an employment tool, your photo can be very helpful to reviewers. Some people may feel uncomfortable about having a picture of themselves on the Internet. If this is the case, leave the photograph space blank, or choose another image in its place, such as a school logo or crest.

Quick Clicks: Adding or Changing Your Photo

1. Click **Tools** on the left hand side navigation bar.

2. Click **Settings.** This will bring up your current personal information and display your current image.

3. On the right hand side next to your photo, click **Edit;** that will bring up the Browse button in the top portion of the application.

4. Click **Browse** and navigate to the image file on your computer (see page 70 for appropriate image file types).

5. Single click on the image file.

6. Click **Open.** You will be returned to the Digital Portfolio application.

7. Click **Save** for the changes to take effect.

8. Click **Close** to complete the process.

Tools: The Directory

The Directory provides a comprehensive, searchable listing of all portfolio community members. Members can also use the Directory to create personalized groups to more quickly and easily communicate and collaborate with a small subset of the larger group.

   The Directory in the JHU Digital Portfolio is a listing of all the members of your specific portfolio community. The directory allows you to easily view and contact these members. Each portfolio community member, student, faculty member, or mentor is listed in this area of the portfolio. You can use the directory to set up groups for your classes, work groups, and cohorts. This feature makes communications with members quick and easy.

How to View a Member's Profile

Members' profiles contain information about their relation to the portfolio community. Which program they are in? Are they faculty members or students? Are they in a degree program or a certificate program? The information available depends on what information the member chooses to provide during the registration process. (Member profiles may be edited at any time.)

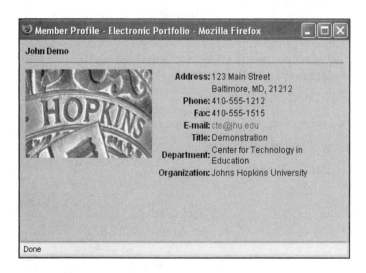

Figure 4.19 Member's Profile

Quick Clicks: Viewing a Member's Profile

1. From the home page, click **Tools** on the main menu.

2. From the Tools main page, click **Directory.**

3. This will automatically bring you to the Directory main page.

4. Use the drop-down menu to choose a Group ("All Members" may be a group).

5. Scroll through the list to find the member whose profile you would like to view.

6. Click on the highlighted name to view the member profile.

A small box will open on the screen, providing you with the member's photo and contact information (depending on the information they provided during the registration process).

Sending E-Mail from the Directory

You can also send e-mail directly to one or more Digital Portfolio members from the Directory. This is a handy feature that allows you to send e-mail from within the portfolio application.

Quick Clicks: E-Mail

If you want to send e-mail to one person:

1. From the home page, click **Tools** on the main menu.

2. From the Tools main page, click **Directory.**

3. This will bring you automatically to the Directory main page.

4. Use the drop-down menu to choose a Group ("All Members" may be a group).

5. Scroll through the list to find the member to whom you'd like to send e-mail.

6. Click on the **E-mail Address** to the right of the person's name.

7. Compose your e-mail as you would normally and click **Send.**

Working through the Directory allows you to send e-mails to groups as well as individuals. When sending e-mails to groups, the process is the same with the exception that the groups must be set up prior to sending the e-mails. Next you will find the directions for setting up and sending e-mails to a group.

Setting Up Groups

Setting up groups within your portfolio directory can be a very helpful and time-saving feature. You can segregate your portfolio community by program, class, semester, cohort, work group, or any other way you wish. Since each user sets up groups individually, the portfolio can truly be your personal tool. Consider making separate groups of friends, associates, or colleagues that you work with on a regular basis. You can set up numerous groups, depending on your definition and requirements for group communication. Members in a group can be set based on people in your course work, your faculty advisors, or people whose opinions you value and seek. And members may be part of multiple groups.

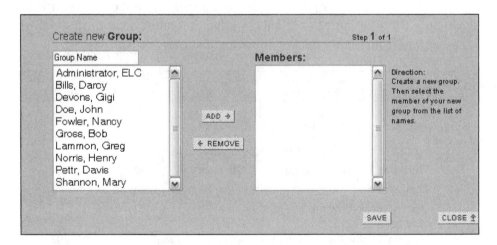

Figure 4.20 Setting Up Groups Feature

Quick Clicks: Creating a New Group

To add or edit the members of a Group in the Directory:

1. From the home page, click **Tools** on the main menu.
2. From the Tools main page, click **Directory.**
3. This will automatically bring you to the Directory main page.
4. Use the drop-down menu to select an existing Group.
5. Click **Create New Group** at the top of the page.
6. A box will open on your screen.
7. Name the Group.
8. If you want to add or remove someone from the group, highlight the appropriate name and click **Add** or **Remove**. To highlight more than one name at a time, hold down the Control button (Shift button on a Mac) and click on each name once.
9. Click **Save.**
10. Click **Close.**

When you have created a group two additional buttons will appear at the top of your screen—Edit Group and Delete Group. Use these buttons to change members of an existing group or to delete a group.

Quick Clicks: Deleting a Group from the Directory

1. From the home page, click **Tools** on the main menu.
2. From the Tools main page, click **Directory.**
3. This will automatically bring you to the Directory main page.
4. Use the drop down menu to select the Group you would like to delete.
5. Click **Delete Group** at the top of the page.
6. A warning will appear. (Warning! This will permanently remove the group.)
7. Click **OK.**

Now that you have your groups set up, you might wish to send them a group e-mail.

Quick Clicks: Sending E-Mail to a Group/Broadcast E-Mail

1.   From the home page, click **Tools** on the main menu.

2.   From the Tools main page, click **Directory.**

3.   This will automatically bring you to the Directory main page.

4.   Use the drop-down menu to choose a Group. ("All Members" may be a group.)

5.   Scroll through the list to find the members to whom you'd like to send e-mail.

6.   Click the check box next to each recipient's name.

7.   Click **Send E-mail** at the bottom of the Directory listing.

8.   Put your cursor in the Subject field and type a message subject.

9.   Put your cursor in the Message field and type your message.

10. Click **Send.**

As with all e-mail sent from within the portfolio, you do not have to have your e-mail application open.

And now that you know how to create folders, save files, create groups, change your personal settings, send broadcast e-mails, add content to your home page, which file type is preferred for use in the portfolio, and more, it is time to look at the standards, artifacts, rationales, and supporting files in Chapter 5.

Chapter 5

Your Working Portfolio

Now that you have logged into your portfolio and entered content into your home page, created a folder or two in your File Cabinet, and uploaded several files, it is now time to look at the heart of your portfolio—linking your content to your selected standards.

As discussed in Part I, one of the primary elements that separates a teaching portfolio from other types of portfolios is its connection to relevant sets of standards. The JHU Digital Portfolio system provides a vehicle for both students of education and in-service professionals to measure their accomplishments and skills against a set of recognized standards or principles. The JHU Digital Portfolio may come to you pre-loaded with specific standard sets such as INTASC (Interstate New Teacher Assessment and Support Consortium) standards, which are recognized nationally as the yardstick by which new teachers should measure their skills.

In addition to the INTASC standards, many pre-service teachers want to highlight their specific content knowledge by using standards developed by professional associations. You may add these additional standard sets at any time during your portfolio development. In some cases, your program or school may have standards that you are required to use. Regardless of the set or sets of standards you wish to include in your portfolio, the process is the same. As a portfolio developer, you may use the pre-loaded standards or add additional standards sets as needed by your program, or as you determine yourself to be helpful.

So What Is a Standard?

Standards are also often referred to as principles. Although slightly different in definition, the terms *principle* and *standard* are often used interchangeably and for the purposes of this manual and the portfolio application, we will consider the terms interchangeable. The term *standard* refers to a set of skills or competencies that a group of recognized experts has determined are necessary for success in the field. You may already be familiar with the INTASC standards or other types of standards. But what really is a standard? Standards are definitions or descriptions that have been written and/or accepted by a recognized oversight organization or have been accepted by the industry or profession through their widespread use as benchmark levels of performance. In the field of education, standards are the yardstick by which teaching skills are measured. It is through the portfolio that a teacher may demonstrate her hard-to-quantify skills such as classroom management and student engagement as well as content knowledge, planning, assessment, and use of technology.

The following is an example of content area principles, in this case Principles for School Mathematics developed by the National Council of Teachers of Mathematics. The six principles for school mathematics describe features of high-quality mathematics education:

1. **Equity.** Excellence in mathematics education requires equity—high expectation and strong support for all students

2. **Curriculum.** A curriculum is more than a collection of activities: it must be coherent, focused on important mathematics, and well articulated across the grades.

3. **Teaching.** Effective mathematics teaching requires understanding what students know and need to learn and then challenging and supporting them to learn it well.

4. **Learning.** Students must learn mathematics with understanding, actively building new knowledge from experience and prior knowledge.

5. **Assessment**. Assessment should support the learning of important mathematics and furnish useful information to both teachers and students.

6. **Technology**. Technology is essential in teaching and learning mathematics; it influences the mathematics that is taught and enhances students' learning.

Adding a New Set of Standards or Principles

Your portfolio application comes to you pre-populated with a specific set of standards. If you wish to add additional standards or course or program objectives in this area, then follow these directions. Standards are entered in the Portfolio domain; more accurately, this is the working portfolio, because this area is visible only to you, the portfolio developer, and those with whom you choose to share it. This is your workspace when you are linking your work to the standards.

You may have up to four sets of standards in your portfolio and there is no limit to the number of individual standards in each set. However, please keep in mind that too many standards sets can make your portfolio lack in focus and purpose. As you maintain your portfolio through the years, it is possible that the relevant standard sets will change. Your portfolio may grow from a student's portfolio with a focus on pre-service standards to a professional's portfolio containing standards for national board certification, state teacher or administrator standards, or national technology standards. And in most cases, old or unused standard sets may be deleted. However, please note that the deletion is permanent and cannot be undone. When standards are deleted, the corresponding interpretations are deleted as well.

To add a new set of standards or principles, click on the Portfolio domain on the left side of your screen and then click on the Add button on the right of Standard Sets.

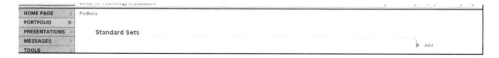

Figure 5.1 Standard Sets Screen

You will see the now familiar screen where you can now add a title for your new set of standards and a description. You will notice the HTML quick editors on the upper right side of the text box. After you have entered the title of the set and a description, please click Save and Close. To add the individual standards, click on the Title of the standard set and then the "Add standard" button on the right. You will again see the familiar gray window and now have an opportunity to title the standard.

Figure 5.2 Adding a Standard/Principle

Quick Clicks: Adding a Standard Set

1. Click **Portfolio.**
2. Click **Add** (next to Standard sets).
3. When you see the gray window, title your new standards and provide a description. Use HTML quick editors if you wish.
4. Click **Save** and then **Close.**

Now, in addition to any pre-loaded standard sets that may have come with your application, you may now maintain your portfolio with up-to-date and appropriate standards for your work now and in the future.

Remember that the portfolio section of your application is not a public space, and in reality, there is little reason to delete any standard sets. No one can view these areas but you, the portfolio developer. You may wish to keep standard sets in this area in the event that you need them later.

Quick Clicks: Adding Individual Standards

1. Click **Portfolio.**
2. Click on the Title of the Standard set.
3. Add a title for the individual standard. (Example: "Standard One")
4. In the text area, enter the exact text of the standard as you wish it to appear in your portfolio.
5. Click **Save** and **Close.**
6. Repeat until each individual standard has been entered.

Interpreting the Standards

Once a set (or sets) of standards has been selected, take some time and study each individual standard. Often standards are written by committees in very "academic" language. Make sure that you understand what each standard means and how it will apply to your education and your work. When you have developed an understanding of the standard, begin to write your personal interpretation of the standard. Your interpretation should be concise and should explain why you think the standard is important and how it will affect your work. It is expected that your interpretation of a standard will change as you gain more experience and your skills grow. You may go in and edit your interpretations of standards at any time.

It is important that you have a clear understanding of each standard you are addressing. As you clarify these standards in your mind you should be able to write your interpretation of the standard in no more than about eight sentences in length. Your interpretation should, above all else, show you understand what, as a teacher, these standards mean to you and your teaching.

The following is an example of a student teacher's interpretation of INTASC Standard Two.

INTASC Standard Two
The teacher understands how children learn and develop, and can provide learning opportunities that support their intellectual, social, and personal development.

Actual Student Interpretation:
The teacher understands that learners' intellectual, social, and personal development influence learning, and she uses instructional strategies which support their various needs and developmental levels. The teacher is sensitive to individual variation within developmental areas; she plays an integral role in the students' development of positive self-concepts by creating opportunities for all students to succeed. The teacher builds upon students' strengths and prior knowledge, and values students' approximations as an opportunity for learning to take hold. The teacher chooses age and developmentally appropriate activities that promote the development of the whole child. The teacher values active engagement by creating learning opportunities which encourage, for example, dialogue, cooperative interaction, and hands-on learning. She further believes that self-assessment is a powerful tool in motivating students to learn, because when students are able to set their own objectives and monitor and evaluate their own progress, they develop insights into themselves and their learning.

Here is another example of a student's interpretation of a standard.

INTASC Principle Ten
The teacher fosters relationships with school colleagues, parents, and agencies in the larger community to support students' learning and well-being.

Actual Student Interpretation:
The teacher values interpersonal relationships with parents, colleagues, community, and external agencies. The teacher realizes that active collaboration with these groups fosters student learning and enhances teaching effectiveness. The teacher understands that a student's family, community, and cultural background effects his/her learning experience, and she uses this knowledge to integrate parents into the classroom structure as an important part of teacher-home partnerships. Furthermore, the teacher participates in school and community activities, believing that her role extends beyond the walls of the classroom.

The Interstate New Teacher Assessment and Support Consortium (INTASC) standards were developed by the Council of Chief State School Officers and member states. Copies may be downloaded from the Council's website at http://www.ccsso.org.

Council of Chief State School Officers. (1992). Model standards for beginning teacher licensing, assessment, and development: A resource for state dialogue. Washington, DC: Author. http://www.ccsso.org/content/pdfs/corestrd.pdf.

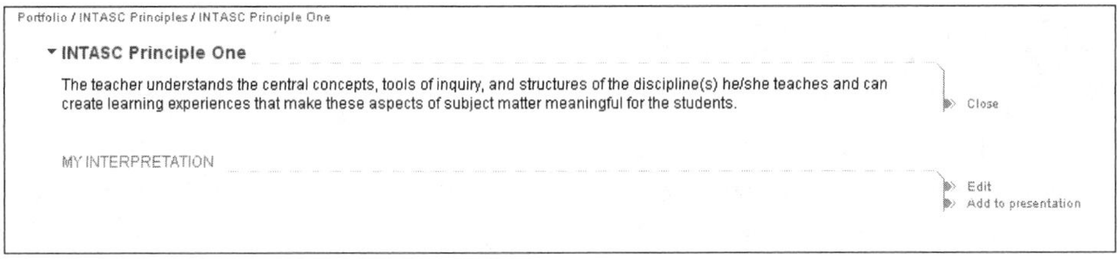

Figure 5.3 Adding Personal Interpretations

Quick Clicks: Adding Your Personal Interpretation to a Standard

1. Click **Portfolio.**
2. Click on the title of the selected standard set.
3. Click on the specific individual standard.
4. Click **Edit** on the right side of the screen opposite My Interpretation.
5. Enter your interpretation of the standard.
6. Click **Save** and **Close** when completed.
7. You may go in and edit your interpretation at any time.

As you read the standards, also read any additional information that might be provided regarding the knowledge, dispositions, and/or performances and expectations associated with the standard. Then, in your own words and in relationship to your field of study, note your personal understanding of the standard.

Here is another example of a personal interpretation of a standard.

> The teacher uses a variety of instructional techniques and strategies to stimulate higher-order thinking and questioning. These strategies may include: independent problem-solving, constructivist learning, group discussion, or cooperative learning. The teacher considers the students' needs and learning outcomes when choosing appropriate instructional strategies. The teacher models critical thinking and provides opportunities for students to participate in oral discourse where they explain, extend, evaluate and challenge their ideas. The teacher uses informal assessment strategies to consider instructional effectiveness and to make adjustments which will best suit the needs of her students.

Artifacts and More

In a somewhat awkward metaphor, the standards in your portfolio are similar to your destination on a road trip. The standards are the place you are traveling to, whereas your artifact rationales and their related supporting files serve as your vehicle and the actual path you take to reach your goals. While there is no right or wrong way to demonstrate your competency of selected standards, there are suggestions and tips that will make your travels easier and more enjoyable.

What Is a Rationale? (Artifact Rationale)

Simply, the rationale is the connection between the standard (including your personal interpretation of the standard) and the actual tangible work that demonstrates your achievement of that standard (the supporting files). The Artifact Rationale provides the context for the supporting files and sets the purpose for the individual files (artifacts). A well-written artifact rationale should contain these elements:

- Identification of the artifact components

- The connection of the artifacts to the specific standard being addressed

- An explanation of the intended purpose of the artifact in instruction and how it was actually used

- The identification of and a discussion of the impact the activity had on student learning and achievement

Because the rationale is the written link between the supporting file(s) (the works you earlier uploaded to your File Cabinet) and the standard, each rationale statement should briefly describe what is included in the artifact, how the artifacts demonstrate your skills and are linked to the standard, and how your artifacts were important to student learning. Written in the first person, it should be brief (6–10 sentences).

The Artifact Rationale is exactly that—it is your justification or reasoning for selecting the specific files you did to demonstrate your attainment of the standards. Therefore, obviously the artifact rationale cannot be written before your supporting files have been identified.

An effective rationale should answer the following questions:

1. Why were the supporting files were chosen?

2. How do the supporting files relate to the standard?

3. How were the supporting files used in instruction?

4. How did the the supporting files affect the learning process?

The artifact rationale is second in importance only to the supporting file itself. This is where your comprehension of the standard and your understanding of how the portfolio elements are interrelated are most evident. As you take some time writing your artifact rationales, be reflective in your thinking. Remember that the artifact rationale is the glue that connects your work to the standard and must clearly convey "I have met this standard because…"

Over a period of several months or years, you may collect dozens of files that could show your achievement of certain standards. Your rationale should explain why the specific supporting files were selected over others. Remember your portfolio is a living document that will grow and change as your education and experiences change your perspectives. You may edit your rationale at any time. Over time, you may find more suitable supporting files to demonstrate your accomplishments; therefore your artifact rationale as well as the corresponding supporting files will change.

Example of an Artifact Rationale:

This student is connecting INTASC Principle Three to a graphic organizer she used in a lesson.

I used this graphic organizer with my on-level sixth graders. I first taught this book to my GT (gifted and talented) students and they caught onto the three disconnected events quickly. When I was contemplating teaching this book to my on-level students, I felt I needed to differentiate my presentation and teaching of the novel. I introduced the triangle before we read the prologue. After reading the prologue together I asked my classes what they thought the three points on the triangle represented. They identified the points as representing the three disconnected events that were introduced in the prologue. They filled in each point and then used it to take notes as they continued to read and learn more about the different characters and plots that were occurring in the novel. This tool worked well with these students because it provided them with a visual representation that they could continually reference as they read *Tuck Everlasting*.

The Interstate New Teacher Assessment and Support Consortium (INTASC) standards were developed by the Council of Chief State School Officers and member states. Copies may be downloaded from the Council's website at http://www.ccsso.org.

Council of Chief State School Officers. (1992). Model standards for beginning teacher licensing, assessment, and development: A resource for state dialogue. Washington, DC: Author. http://www.ccsso.org/content/pdfs/corestrd.pdf.

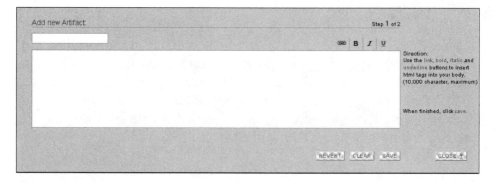

Figure 5.4 Adding an Artifact

Quick Clicks: Adding an Artifact Rationale

1. Click **Portfolio** on the main menu to be taken to the Portfolio main page.
2. Click on the appropriate highlighted **Standard Name** to be taken to the main screen for the Standard.
3. Click **Add** to the right of the appropriate Artifact Rationale to open a gray text box.
4. Enter your artifact rationale.
5. Click **Save** and then **Close.**
   a. **Revert** returns your text to its previous state, prior to the last time you saved it.
   b. **Clear** deletes your interpretation, allowing you start over.

Quick Clicks: Deleting an Artifact Rationale

1. From the home page, click **Portfolio** on the main menu.
2. You will automatically be taken to the Portfolio main page.
3. Click on the appropriate highlighted **Standard Name.**
4. You will automatically be taken to the main screen for the Standard.
5. Click on the appropriate highlighted **standard.**
6. You will automatically be taken to the main screen for the standard.
7. Click **Delete** to the right of the appropriate highlighted Artifact name.
8. A warning message will appear on the screen. (Warning! This will remove the artifact and all associated content. This action is permanent.)
9. Click **OK.**

Evidence supporting a member's attainment of an educational principle is crucial to the portfolio process. In the case of the digital portfolio, you will add electronic evidence (documents, images, and video) to support your knowledge of and experience with each standard. The Artifact Rationale is the "glue" that ties the supporting evidence to the standard.

Artifacts

As we drill down through the portfolio from the top to the bottom the progression looks like this:

1. *Standard* (the skill objective)

    a. *Interpretation of Standard*
       (the objective from your personal perspective)

        i. *Artifact Rationale* (the narrative justification for linking the chosen files to the standard)

            1. *Supporting File*(s) (text or images that serve as proof of competency)

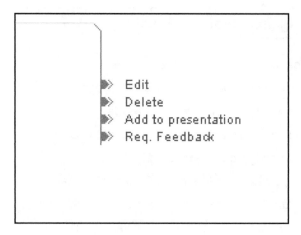

Figure 5.5 Function Buttons

There are several buttons to the right of your Artifact Rationale labeled Edit, Delete, Copy, Add to Presentation, Request Feedback. We have already talked about the Edit and Delete buttons. The Copy button allows you to copy the artifact rationale to another area of your portfolio without the need to re-enter it.

Often, one rationale may be used to link several files to one standard. This is perfectly acceptable and encouraged as long as the files complement one another. Often uploaded as individual files, these pieces of supporting evidence combine to form a rich and complex artifact.

The Three Categories of Artifacts

As mentioned in Part I of this guide, there are three categories of artifacts (supporting files) that you can collect and add to your File Cabinet in preparation for inclusion in your portfolio.

Authentic Evidence or Documentation

These include examples of things that you actually did—lessons you developed and implemented, tests/essays you scored, newsletters you sent home, learning stations you created, as well as examples of student work, projects, models, and assessments. The evidence can be the paper documents, photographs of 3-D projects, or photos or videos illustrating cooperative learning, using manipulatives, or of student presentations.

Explanations or Reflections

This category includes teacher-developed narratives (oral or written) that provide context and clarification of the artifact—whether it is an event, an activity, or a product. Explanations or reflections can be Journal entries related to an incident, notes jotted at the bottom of a lesson plan about modifications for next time, or formal rationales developed for each artifact.

Validation Entries or Observations

These represent a third-party view of an event or product. Formal observations and evaluations are found in this category; that is, someone else is providing verification of what you have identified as an artifact. They are usually not used as stand-alone artifacts, but help support the developer's case regarding a quality issue and can provide additional information from another point of view.

A well-developed portfolio contains examples from each of the different categories. You might want to make a grid as you select and identify artifacts and make certain that you have representation from each of the categories outlined above.

Remember, files must be in your File Cabinet before they can be added to your portfolio.

Figure 5.6 Adding Artifacts

Quick Clicks: Adding Artifacts/Supporting Evidence

1. From the home page, click **Portfolio** on the main menu.

2. You will be taken automatically to the Portfolio main page.

3. Click on the appropriate highlighted **Standard Name.**

4. You will be taken automatically to the main screen for the standard.

5. Click on the appropriate highlighted **Standard.**

6. You will be taken automatically to the main screen for the standard.

7. Click on the appropriate **Artifact Rationale.**

8. Click **Open** and then **Add** to the right of the words Supporting Files.

9. A gray box will appear on the screen.

10. Place your cursor in the small text box and type a name for the Evidence.

11. Click on the icon for the **File Cabinet** and select your Supporting File.

12. Place your cursor in the large text box, and type a description for the Supporting Evidence.

13. Click **Save** and then **Close.**

14. **Revert** returns your text to its previous state, prior to the last time you saved it.

15. **Clear** deletes your entry, allowing you start over.

Quick Clicks: Editing Supporting Evidence

1. From the home page, click **Portfolio** on the main menu.

2. You will be taken automatically to the Portfolio main page.

3. Click on the appropriate highlighted **Standard Name.**

4. You will be taken automatically to the main screen for the Standard.

5. Click on the appropriate highlighted **standard.**

6. You will be taken automatically to the main screen for the standard.

7. Click on the appropriate highlighted **Artifact Rationale.**

8. Click **Open** and then **Edit** to the right of the Supporting Evidence you would like to edit.

9. A gray box will appear on the screen with the current file name and description.

10. Place your cursor in the description or name field and type your edits.

11. Click **Save** and then **Close.**

12. **Revert** returns your text to its previous state, prior to the last time you saved it.

13. **Clear** deletes your entry, allowing you start over.

This section of the portfolio is where you will spend the majority of your time and effort. A reviewer of your portfolio should see an unambiguous connection running from the standard to your interpretation of that standard to your artifact rationale and then to your supporting files. These links are the strong evidence that you clearly understand and have achieved the objective; this is the heart of your portfolio. An outline of your portfolios may look similar to the graphic in Figure 5.7.

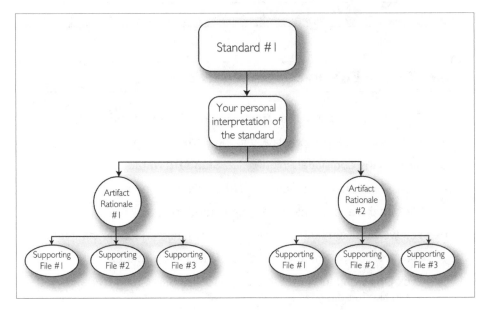

Figure 5.7 Outline of a Portfolio

Beginning work on a portfolio is often a daunting task. Students might have a difficult time believing that they will produce a sufficient quantity of work or have an adequate variety of file types to complete their portfolios. This is rarely the case. Much more common is the student who includes more items than necessary in his portfolio and has much more of a challenge selecting appropriate files to support standards. If you find yourself having trouble determining which files to include or how many, ask your peers and instructors for advice. In most cases, it is not only acceptable, but preferred, to have two to three artifact rationales and linking collections of supporting files for each standard. While it may be tempting to include a great quantity of your work in your portfolio that you uploaded into your File Cabinet, it is not necessary. Remember that your portfolio should contain examples of your *best* work that supports the standard, not *all* your work. Pare your supporting files down until you think you have a manageable sample of your best work. You may end up with several hundred files in your File Cabinet, but only use 20 or so in your portfolio.

It is relatively easy to collect samples of your work in a folder. It is more difficult, but much more meaningful, to connect these samples of work to your personal understanding of professional standards and to explain to your reviewer why you felt the collected files were the best examples of your work. This is a primary function of a teaching portfolio.

It is important to remember that everything you have added to your portfolio is visible only to you, the portfolio developer. You control who sees your portfolio and when. There are two primary ways to allow others to view your portfolio: through the Request Feedback button and the Presentation mode. The Request Feedback mode allows others to provide critical commentary on your portfolio, during the development phase, whereas the Presentation mode allows you to publish a version of your portfolio which can be distributed through the Internet or alternative media. We will talk more about these features in the Chapter 6.

Chapter 6

Sharing Your Portfolio with Others—Using Feedback, the Message Center and the Presentation Features

Overview of the Feedback System

Much of the work that goes into developing a professional portfolio is inevitably done in isolation. Just as no one can review your master's thesis or term paper while it's a work in progress, access to your portfolio is limited to you alone until *you* decide otherwise. No one can check up your progress or provide guidance without your consent. (An instructor could require you to give access as part of a course requirement, but more about this later.) This ability to control access to portfolio content is critical, as first drafts of artifact rationales, interpretations, and other written narratives are often "not ready for prime time." But at some point, bringing trusted friends and advisors into the process is also critical to ensure that you are on the right track. That's where the request feedback function comes in. Next to each piece of content in your portfolio, there is a request feedback link that allows you to invite friends, family, colleagues, fellow students, or faculty advisors to review portions of your portfolio and provide feedback.

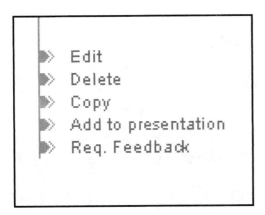

Figure 6.1 Request Feedback Button

This process allows you to grant temporary access to all or part of your portfolio to selected members of the portfolio community or guests for the purpose of requesting help, guidance, or constructive criticism to improve your working portfolio. The feedback request will stay active for a period of 14 days, after which access to the specified section(s) will once again close. Therefore, responses to your requests for feedback will be timely.

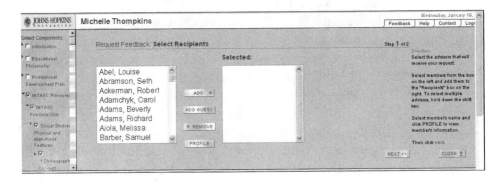

Figure 6.2 Request Feedback Screen

Quick Clicks: Requesting Feedback

Throughout the course of your work on the Digital Portfolio, you may want to request that colleagues or fellow students critique your progress and provide feedback. The process for requesting feedback is similar no matter where you are within the application. To request feedback on a home page content element:

1. From the home page, click **Req Feedback** next to one of the content areas.

2. A gray feedback request box will open on your screen.

3. Use the check boxes on the left hand side of the screen to choose the areas of the Portfolio on which you would like to receive feedback.

4. Next, highlight the names of the people you would like to review your work, and click **Add**. To highlight more than one name at a time, hold down the Control button (Shift button on a Mac) and click on each name once.

5. When you are finished adding names, click **Next.**

6. Type a message to the people from whom you are requesting feedback. (Remember that the same message will go to everyone you added to the feedback list.)

7. Click **Send Request**.

How to Request Feedback

By clicking the Request Feedback link located to the right of any piece of content in your portfolio, you will open the feedback screen. This is where you select the sections of your portfolio you would like to have reviewed. This screen includes an outline of your portfolio in the upper-left corner, shown in Figure 6.3 on page 106.

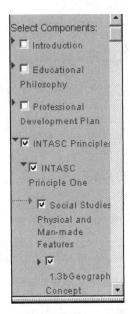

Figure 6.3 Feedback Screen

As you add more items to your working portfolio, those additional items will appear in the outline. Placing a check mark in the small box next to a particular item in the outline will open up that item for viewing by your advisors (who are selected in the next step). For example, you may want your introduction and educational philosophy to be available for review, but perhaps your professional development plan isn't quite ready. You would place a check mark next to the first two items, and leave the box next to professional development plan empty. Remember, whatever you want reviewed should have a check mark beside it, and whatever you want to remain private should not.

Clicking the small triangles next to each section will reveal the next layer in the outline, allowing you more granular control over which elements you would like to include in your feedback request. For example, if you click that you would like feedback on all of Standard One, then all artifacts and files below Standard One will be available to your reviewers. But, if you decide that you would like to keep Artifact Rationale 2 private for now, just un-check the box next to Artifact Rationale 2.

Once you have indicated which elements should be available as part of this feedback request, your next step is to determine from *whom* you would like to request feedback. Select the recipients of your feedback request. At the top of the screen, to the right of your outline, is a list of all students and faculty registered in your Digital Portfolio community.

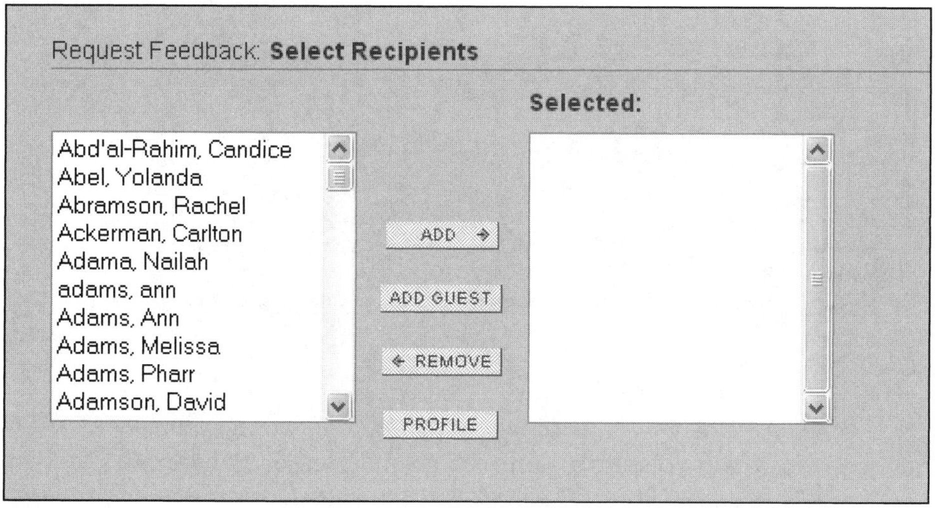

Figure 6.4 Select Recipients Screen

You can request feedback from others in your community by selecting a name from the left, and clicking Add to move the name to the right into the list of recipients. Each person whose name is added to the box on the right side will receive your feedback request. To remove someone from that list, simply highlight the name and click Remove.

You can also request feedback from someone outside your portfolio community by clicking Add Guest and completing the short form. Once you've added guests, they will appear in your Digital Portfolio community list for future use. Once you are done adding recipients, click Next.

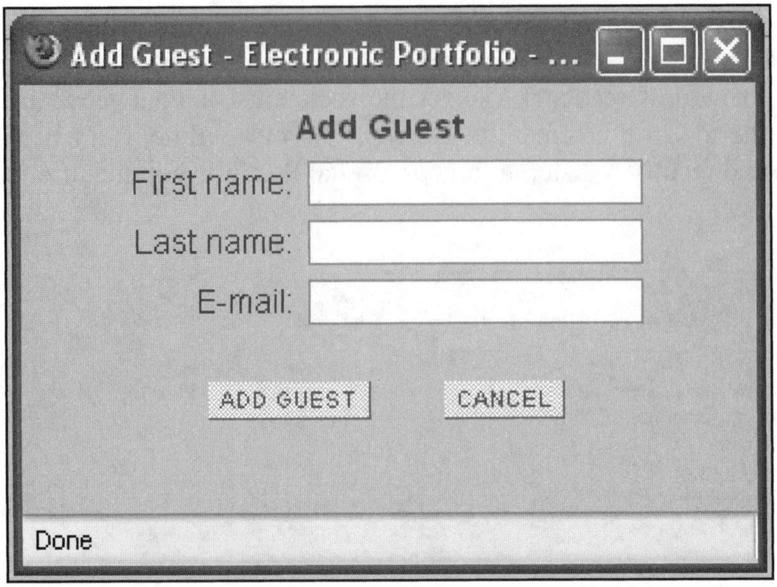

Figure 6.5 Add Guest Screen

To ensure that the people you are requesting feedback from understand what you are asking of them, please include a note that explains the content you are asking them to review, as well what type of critique you would like, and a date by which you need their response.

A sample message: *"Thanks in advance for taking the time to look at these items from my portfolio. I feel pretty good about the interpretation, but the artifact rationale and the supporting file is giving me some trouble. Do you think this is appropriate here, or should I find something else to demonstrate my mastery of this principle?"*

Figure 6.6 Message to Reviewers

Once you have finished writing your message, click Send Request. If the recipients are members of your portfolio community, a new feedback request will appear in their message center the next time they log into the system, along with a link to review the items you have included in the request. For guest recipients, an e-mail will be sent that includes a guest login and password and a link to your portfolio content.

When you request feedback from a member of your portfolio community or an outside guest, please be aware that these people will have access to your portfolio (only the elements that you selected for feedback) for a period of only two weeks. After that time period they will no longer be able to see your portfolio elements. However, because the portfolio application is dynamic and your colleagues providing feedback will be viewing your portfolio in real time, any changes you make to the elements opened to them will be visible.

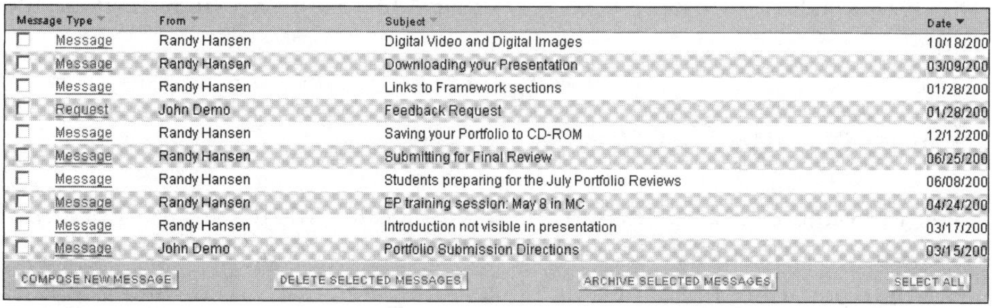

Message Type ▼	From ▼	Subject ▼	Date ▼
Message	Randy Hansen	Digital Video and Digital Images	10/18/200
Message	Randy Hansen	Downloading your Presentation	03/09/200
Message	Randy Hansen	Links to Framework sections	01/28/200
Request	John Demo	Feedback Request	01/28/200
Message	Randy Hansen	Saving your Portfolio to CD-ROM	12/12/200
Message	Randy Hansen	Submitting for Final Review	06/25/200
Message	Randy Hansen	Students preparing for the July Portfolio Reviews	06/08/200
Message	Randy Hansen	EP training session: May 8 in MC	04/24/200
Message	Randy Hansen	Introduction not visible in presentation	03/17/200
Message	John Demo	Portfolio Submission Directions	03/15/200

COMPOSE NEW MESSAGE | DELETE SELECTED MESSAGES | ARCHIVE SELECTED MESSAGES | SELECT ALL

Figure 6.7 Message Screen

It will be helpful to your peers from whom you are requesting feedback to be as specific as possible about what you are looking for. If you are looking for advice on the appropriateness of a particular supporting file, then send them not only the file, but the artifact rationale and your interpretation of the standard. These items together will give them a more complete picture of your work. If you are looking for someone to proofread your near-final presentation, then make sure those are the instructions in your message.

Your portfolio allows you to capture and maintain these messages from your colleagues regarding feedback. These messages can be particularly interesting to review when you are constructing a portfolio over a long period of time. You can look back at comments you received in the beginning of the process and compare them to the level of feedback you received later in your program.

Giving Feedback to Others

If you are the recipient of a feedback request from another Digital Portfolio member, you will be alerted with a message just below your photo on the home page the next time you log in to the portfolio system. The message will include an outline of the content that the sender of the feedback request has given you access to, along with a button that says Give Feedback. Clicking on this button will open a new window into the requesting person's portfolio. The new window will include an outline of the content they would like you to review on the top left, and a feedback text box for you to provide the comments on the top right. The bottom of the window will display the actual content you select from the outline. This allows you to review the comment and provide feedback above as appropriate. When you're ready to submit your comments, click Send Feedback below the text box. To close the text box, click Exit in the upper right corner.

The Message Center

The Message Center is the communications hub of the Digital Portfolio, providing community members with a quick snapshot of new and existing portfolio messages, feedback messages received, and requests for feedback. In addition, the Messages area allows application users to compose and send messages to other members of the community.

The ability to send and receive feedback is only one of the features of the integrated message center. Clicking on Messages from the home page takes you into the portfolio system's Message Center. The purpose of the message center is to provide a convenient place for managing and archiving all portfolio-related communications. This includes two primary types of messages: (1) feedback requests (described in detail in the previous sections) and (2) portfolio messages, which include all other messages sent between and among portfolio community members that do not originate from the Request Feedback system.

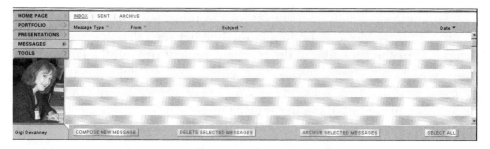

Figure 6.8 Message Center

Upon entering the message center, new messages or feedback requests that have arrived since your last login will be highlighted in a bold, red font. The first column in the message header will tell if the message is a feedback request (request), feedback someone has sent you in response to your request (feedback), or a normal message not associated with the feedback system (message). Subsequent columns in the header include the sender's name, the subject of the message, and the sent date.

Quick Clicks: Reading Your Messages

1. From the home Page, click **Messages** on the main menu

2. You will automatically be taken to the Messages area within the Digital Portfolio.

3. To read a message, click on either the **Message Type**, **From** or **Subject** line. The text of the selected message will appear on the lower half of the page.

To compose a new message from the message center, look for the Compose New Message button on the line between the message headers (top half of the screen) and the message content (bottom half). Also, on this line you'll find buttons that allow you to delete and archive messages (after first selecting one or more messages by clicking the check box to the left of the message header).

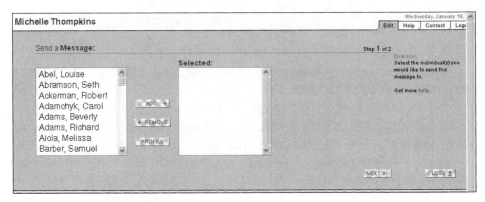

Figure 6.9 Send a Message: Step 1

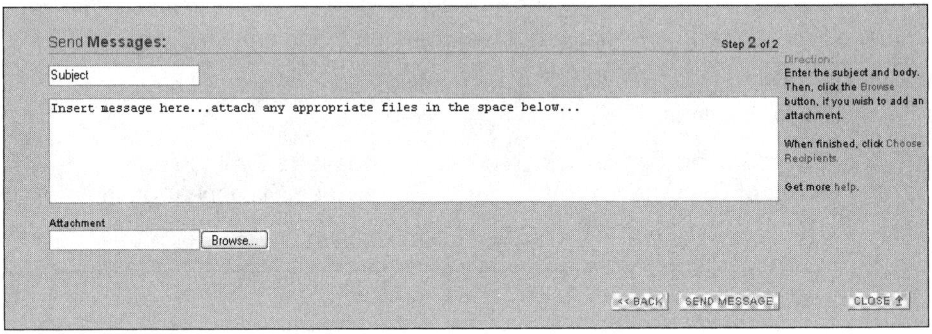

Figure 6.10 Send a Message: Step 2

The difference between deleting and archiving is important to consider. Deleting a message permanently removes it from your message center. If you think you may want to refer to the message later, or use it to demonstrate how the feedback you received influenced your professional growth over time, you should archive the message instead of deleting it. To view your archived messages, click the Archive tab just above your message center. Next to the archive tab, you'll also find a Sent tab that allows you to review messages you have sent to others.

Quick Clicks: Sending a Message

To compose and send a message to any member of the portfolio community:

1. From the home page, click **Messages** on the main menu.

2. You will automatically be taken to the Messages areas within the Digital Portfolio.

3. Click **Compose New Message**

4. Highlight the names of the people you would like to send the message to, and click **Add**. To highlight more than one name at a time, hold down the Control button (Shift button on a Mac) and click on each name once.

5. Click **Next.**

6. Place your cursor in the subject box, and type a subject for your message.

7. Then place your cursor in the Message box, and type your message.

8. If you want to attach a file to your message, put your cursor in the attachment box, click **Browse**, locate the file you want to attach, then click **Open**. The dialog box will close and the file path will be visible in the Browse text box.

9. When you are ready to send the message, click **Send Message.**

10. **Back** returns you to the previous page.

11. **Close** returns you to your In Box *without sending the message.*

Note: Requests for feedback are composed and sent from the area of the portfolio on which you'd like feedback. They are not sent from the Messages area. You may request feedback on multiple areas of your portfolio in one message; simply check all the content you wish to include.

Quick Clicks: Deleting Messages

You can delete messages from the Message area at any time:

1. From the home page, click **Messages** on the main menu.
2. You will automatically be taken to the Messages area within the Digital Portfolio.
3. Use the check box next to each message to select the message
4. Click **Delete Selected Messages.**

Note: To delete all messages, click **Select All**, then **Delete Selected Messages.**

Quick Clicks: Sort Messages by Type, From, Subject, and Date

In Box messages can be ordered according to Message Type (message, request, response to request), From (sender's name), or Subject Line (alphabetical).

1. From the home page, click **Messages** on the main menu.
2. You will be taken automatically to the Messages area within the Digital Portfolio.
3. To sort the messages, click on either the **Message Type**, **From,** or **Subject** line.

Messages will be sorted and displayed according to your preference.

Three Ways to View Feedback

As previously discussed, the feedback you receive from peers and faculty while developing your portfolio is important for two key reasons. First, the feedback you receive can help you to identify areas where your portfolio could be stronger. Critical, constructive comments can be invaluable in improving the overall quality of your portfolio. Second, feedback can help you to document your professional growth over time.

Ideally, a portfolio should not be simply a summative snapshot that highlights your strengths at a given point in time. A more effective portfolio demonstrates growth over time, providing some evidence how you have embraced a process of continuous improvement. Your portfolio feedback can help provide this evidence.

With this in mind, there are three unique ways to view the feedback you have received from your cast of formal and informal advisors:

1. As described above, you can simply read the feedback in your message center and archive it for future reference.

2. Each message you receive will include a Correspondence Log link (see Figure 6.12) that provides you with a sequential log of all correspondence between you and the sender of the message. This is useful for reviewing all feedback from a particular advisor in one quick, easy view.

3. And finally, a more context-driven way of viewing portfolio feedback is to click the Feedback tab in the top-right corner of your screen from anywhere within your working portfolio. This will give you a full listing of all feedback received that specifically pertains to the section of the portfolio that you are currently viewing.

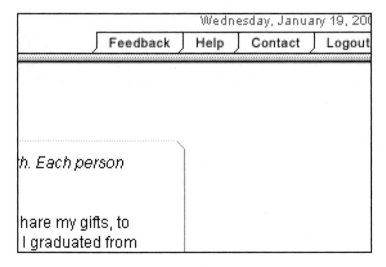

Figure 6.11 Feedback Tab

The Correspondence Log

This feature allows you to see all the correspondence you have exchanged with an individual, such as an instructor or a peer. It can be especially valuable when you are involved in a protracted discussion about a portfolio matter. You easily see the progression of the conversation over several months or even years.

Quick Clicks: Correspondence Log

1. Go into the Message Center by clicking **Messages** on the navigation bar at the left of the screen.

2. Select one of the messages you have in your mailbox by clicking on the blue words under message type or on the sender's name.

3. A split screen appears and your message is in the bottom half of the screen. In order to see the correspondence log, you just click on the tab.

4. The Correspondence Log will appear in a pop-up window.

5. To get back to your electronic portfolio, just click the **Exit** tab in the upper right hand corner of the window.

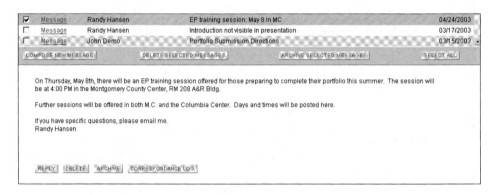

Figure 6.12 Correspondence Log

As you are beginning your portfolio development, take some time to experiment with the Message Center. Send messages to other members of your community and get accustomed to the idea of receiving critical feedback. Your peers and colleagues have much to contribute to your portfolio; they have had similar experiences and are developing portfolios themselves. From within the Message Center you may compose new messages to send to other community members.

Presentations

Up to now, we have discussed the functionality and development of the working portfolio independent of others' ability to view your work without your requesting feedback. Yet, once you have your working portfolio developed to a state where you would like to share with others, what do you do? How can others, such as potential employers, view your work? The portfolio system allows you to select components, or your portfolio as a whole, you wish to have displayed in your presentation. The portfolio system will generate a dynamic Web site displaying those items that you selected, generating a URL unique to your site.

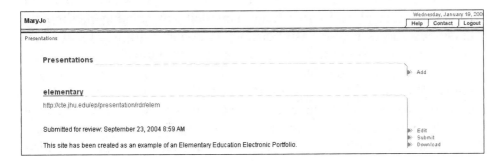

Figure 6.13 Presentations Screen

Since your presentation site is dynamically created when someone visits your Web address (URL), your Web site visitor will always get the latest version of your work. That is, when you make changes to your portfolio (such as update your résumé, modify your educational philosophy, or include additional supporting evidence for a standard) these changes will automatically appear in your presentation site. This also eliminates the need to constantly review your presentation sites to verify if all information is accurate and up to date.

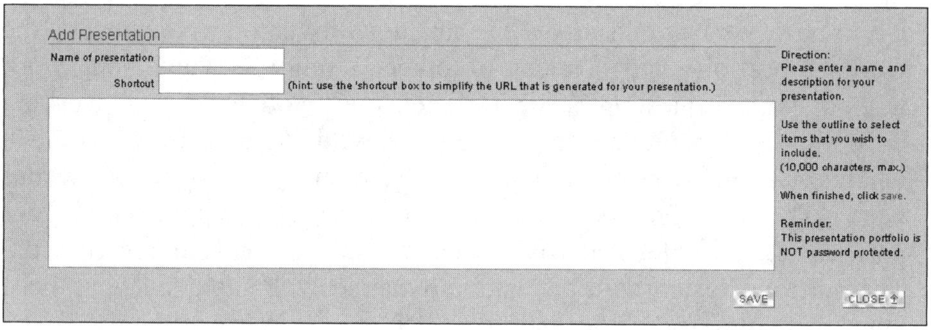

Figure 6.14 Add Presentation

You can include any or all of the elements of your working portfolio in your presentation. However, the simplicity of creating presentation portfolios allows you to easily customize public portfolios to suit your audience. You can use the dynamic application to create presentation to meet many needs. And since the portfolio presentation feature creates a unique Web site for your portfolio that is not password-protected, you can distribute this URL via e-mail or include it on your printed résumé. You can include any or all of the content in your working portfolio in a presentation portfolio and you may use the same content in multiple presentation portfolios.

Once you create your presentation, you can share the URL. This URL becomes your unique Web site hosting your electronic portfolio. The URL can be distributed in your résumé or curriculum vitae, on business cards, or in your e-mail signature.

How to Create a New Presentation

From your working portfolio, click on Presentations from the left-hand side navigation menu. You will need to create a name for the presentation. This will not be seen by others, but will help you to identify and organize your various presentations.

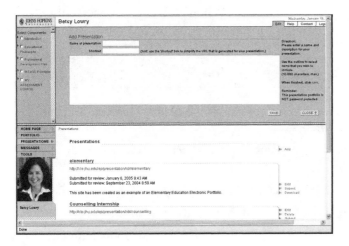

Figure 6.15 Creating a Presentation

You must now create a Shortcut for this presentation. The shortcut must be unique to each presentation and will be displayed in the Web site generated by the portfolio system.

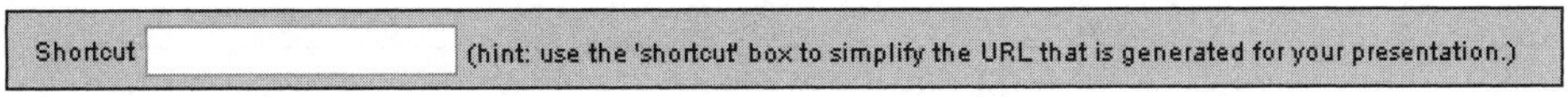

> Shortcut [   ] (hint: use the 'shortcut' box to simplify the URL that is generated for your presentation.)

Figure 6.16 Creating a Shortcut

With each portfolio presentation you create, you may write a brief introduction to welcome or describe the purpose of your Web site for visitors. This allows you the opportunity to make viewers of your portfolio feel they are looking at your best work, created just for them.

Now that you have named your presentation and written a brief introduction, it is time to select which elements you would like to include in your portfolio presentation. On the left side, in the blue shaded area, select those items you wish to include in your presentation by clicking on the box next to its name. When you are finished, click on Save. Voila, you have created a formal presentation of your portfolio!

Quick Clicks: Adding a Presentation

Adding a Presentation, including some or all of the elements in your Digital Portfolio, is quick and easy.

1. From the Digital Portfolio home page, click **Presentations** on the main menu.

2. This will take you to the main Presentation page.

3. Click **Add** to the right of the word Presentations at the top of the page.

4. Place the cursor in the Presentation name field and type a name for your new Presentation (remember to choose a name that others will recognize).

5. Place your cursor in the Presentation description field and type a description (again, remember to use a description that others will recognize).

6. Click **Save** and then **Close.**

Your newly created presentation will appear in the bottom section of the Presentations screen, including an active link of the URL for viewing the Web site, the introduction you wrote for the Web site, and functions to edit or delete the presentation on the right hand side.

Reminder: The presentation Web sites are dynamically generated, so updates and changes to your working portfolio will be reflected in your presentation Web sites. If you make *additions* to your portfolio, add additional standards, artifact rationales, or supporting evidence and would like those new additions to appear in your portfolio, you must edit your presentation to include these new components.

How to Edit Your Presentation

After your presentation has been created, you can go back and make changes without affecting the URL or the Web site people would visit to see your portfolio. You can edit your presentation to update your introduction, include additional standards or artifacts, or remove standards or artifacts. If you have added additional components to your working portfolio, you will need to select these components to be displayed in your presentation site.

As a reminder, if you add new content to your working portfolio and wish to add it to an existing presentation as well, you must edit the presentation to include it. If you delete elements from your working portfolio that are currently part of a presentation, they will be deleted from your presentation as well.

Sometimes it is easier to modify an existing presentation rather than create a new presentation. This action will not create a new URL or ask you to create a new name for your presentation. Simply go to Presentations and then click the Edit button next to the presentation you wish to edit. Make your changes and make sure that you save the revised presentation.

Quick Clicks: Editing a Presentation

1. From the Digital Portfolio home page, click **Presentations** on the main menu.

2. This will take you to the main Presentation page.

3. Click **Edit** to the right of the highlighted Presentation name. (Or, just click on the name itself. Both actions will open a small gray edit box on your screen.)

4. Use the check boxes and tabs on the left hand side of the screen to edit the elements of the Portfolio you add to the Presentation.

5. Place the cursor in the Presentation name field and, if necessary, type a new name for your Presentation.

6. Place your cursor in the Presentation description field and, if necessary, type a new description for your Presentation.

7. Click **Save** and then **Close.**

At times it may be necessary to delete existing presentations. Please be aware that this action is permanent and cannot be reversed. Simply go to the presentation domain and click the Delete button next to the presentation you wish to delete.

Quick Clicks: Deleting a Presentation

1. From the Digital Portfolio Home page, click **Presentations** on the main menu.

2. This will take you to the main Presentation page.

3. Click **Delete** to the right of the presentation you would like to delete.

4. A warning will appear on the screen. (Warning! This will remove the presentation. This action is permanent.)

5. If you still want to delete the presentation, click **OK.**

How to Navigate Through a Presentation

Visitors to your presentation Web site will be able to navigate and explore your portfolio through several easy methods.

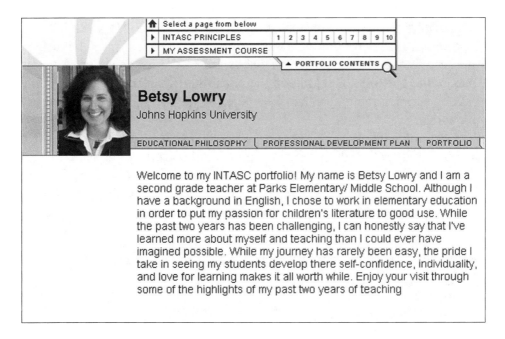

Figure 6.17 Portfolio Contents

The upper right-hand navigation links, listed as Portfolio Contents, allows visitors to quickly access the standards portion of the site. Visitors can quickly navigate directly to one of your standards, interpretations, or artifacts by clicking on the corresponding number. If you have included additional standards in your portfolio, they will also be listed and accessible from this navigation menu.

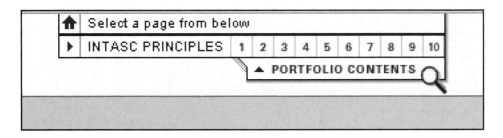

Figure 6.18 Paging in Portfolio Contents

To peruse the portfolio page by page, visitors will click on the forward or backward buttons (see Figure 6.18 on page 123). Clicking on the arrows will page forward or backward to the next part or previous part of the portfolio. Clicking on the portfolio owner's name will quickly take visitors directly to the Web sites home page with introductory paragraph.

Additional features of the presentation interface are the ability for visitors to alter the font size of the portfolio text or to print selections of the portfolio. By simply clicking on the up or down arrows, visitors can increase or decrease the size of the font to make the text easier to read. Printing pages from the portfolio must be done from the page itself. Click on the word Print or on the print icon.

Figure 6.19 Font Size and Print

Quick Clicks: Navigating Through a Presentation

There are three ways to navigate through a presentation: page by page, using the portfolio contents tab at the top of the page, or using the tabs underneath your name.

In order to navigate through a presentation linearly:

1. From the Digital Portfolio home page, click **Presentations** on the main menu.

2. This will take you to the main Presentation page.

3. Click on the **URL** of the Presentation you would like to view linearly.

4. The presentation will open in a separate, smaller window.

5. On the bottom of the page you will notice a large arrow point to the right.

6. Click on the arrow once to proceed to the next page of the Presentation.

7. Continue clicking the arrow to proceed through each page of
    the Presentation.

In order to navigate through a presentation using the tabs under your name:

1. From the DP home page, click **Presentations** on the main menu.

2. This will take you to the main Presentation page.

3. Click on the **URL** of the Presentation you would like to view linearly.

4. The presentation will open in a separate, smaller window.

5. Click on the appropriate tab to view that section of the portfolio.
    (**Note:** Only those sections of the Portfolio that you have added to the
    Presentation will be viewable.)

6. Once in a particular section of the Presentation, navigate using the
    linear arrow at the bottom of the page (page by page) or by clicking on
    highlighted content.

Note: The Portfolio Contents Tab in a Presentation works exactly the same
way as the tab in the Portfolio area. Click on the arrows to expand or contract
your choices, and on the numbers or principle descriptions to open those pages
automatically.

Do you ever get tired of reading things on a computer screen? To
make the review of your portfolio easier on the eyes, you can simply
enlarge the font size on the screen with one click of your mouse. Font
size is an important factor in determining readability and comprehension.
The Presentation component of the Digital Portfolio allows members to
change the font size of presentations to accommodate their readers.

Quick Clicks: Increase/Reduce Font Size

To increase or decrease font size within a Presentation:

1. From the Digital Portfolio home page, click **Presentations** on the
    main menu.

2. This will take you to the main Presentation page.

3. Click on the **URL** of the Presentation you would like to modify.

4. The presentation will open in a separate, smaller window.

5. On the bottom of the page you will notice the words Font Size followed by an up arrow and a down arrow.

6. Click the up arrow to increase the presentation's font size and the down arrow to reduce the presentation's font size.

Note: Font size will stay the same even after you have closed the presentation window.

Despite the ease of reviewing a portfolio on your computer screen, you might want a printed copy. You might wish to include a printed copy with a hard copy of your résumé, or send a printed copy to someone who may have limited technology access. Whatever the reason, printing a copy of your portfolio presentation is a helpful feature.

Quick Clicks: Print Your Presentation

1. From the Digital Portfolio home page, click **Presentations** on the main menu.

2. This will take you to the main Presentations page.

3. Click on the **URL** of the Presentation you would like to print.

4. The presentation will open in a separate, smaller window.

5. Click **Print** (or the printer icon) on the bottom of the page.

6. A dialog box will open on your screen, presenting various printing options.

7. Click **OK** in the dialog box.

Publishing to a CD or Other Media Source

This feature of the Digital Portfolio will allow portfolio owners to download a copy of their portfolio presentation to their local computer. Once on your local computer, you can use the site without an Internet connection or burn the presentation to a CD-ROM.

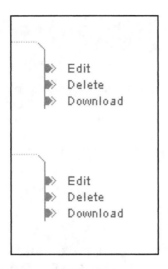

Figure 6.20 Download Feature

You have the ability to create up to five different presentations, but you can download as many presentations as you would like. Downloading enables you to save copies of presentations you no long want to keep active but would like to delete to make room for a different presentation, or to keep various copies of your portfolio in different stages of development or different iterations of your portfolio. It is up to you.

Through the download process, you also have the ability to download one, several, or all the files located within your File Cabinet. You can do this for several reasons: backing up your files, sharing files with others, or making room for new files in your File Cabinet by saving unused files. After you save a copy of your files, you can delete them from your File Cabinet.

There are several steps to the process, but when you are done you will have a zipped folder containing all the files necessary to backup your File Cabinet, present your portfolio without Internet connection, or save the presentation to a CD-ROM. Once downloaded onto your computer, you will need to unzip this folder to gain access to your files or your presentation. You will need a program to unzip your files. If you don't have a program to extract these files, refer to page 67 in Chapter 4 for more information.

> ## Quick Clicks: Creating a CD-ROM of Your Portfolio Presentation
>
> The first step is for you to create a Presentation of your portfolio that includes all components of the portfolio that you want others to view. Once you create and save your presentation, you will see it displayed at the bottom of the Presentation section, complete with the title, URL, and the introduction you wrote when creating the presentation. On the right side of the presentation are several options: edit, delete, and download.
>
> 1. Click **Download** to begin the process of saving your portfolio.
>
> 2. Once you click **Download**, you will get notification that the application is beginning to start the process.
>
> 3. Depending on the size of your portfolio presentation, the process could be quick or take a few minutes. Be patient; you will be notified when to proceed.
>
> 4. Once the application has prepared your presentation, you will get a notification screen giving details about the download process.
>
> 5. You will be notified of the filename, the size, and estimated download times. This window must remain open during the entire process. The next step is going to be deciding where to save your presentation.
>
> 6. The **Save As** dialog box will automatically open for you. Here you can choose where to save the zipped file (A) and determine the filename for the presentation (B). The filename will be pre-set by the portfolio application itself with your name and a presentation number. You can change the filename, but be sure to write down the new title and location where you are going to save.
>
> 7. After selecting a location to save and your filename, click on **Save.** The downloading process will take a few moments, but you will be notified when it is complete.
>
> 8. The **Download Complete** dialog box will appear when your presentation has been completely saved onto your computer.
>
> 9. Click **Close.**

You have now saved your presentation! You will see this type of icon with the filename in the site where you saved your presentation.

You have downloaded a zipped folder containing your digital portfolio presentation. All the files you need to run your presentation without an Internet connection or to burn your presentation onto a portable media (CD-ROM or DVD) are there. Double-click on the icon to extract the files. (You will need an application to extract the files. Check to see if your computer has an unzip application installed by double-clicking on the filename.) Once you've extracted the files, you have complete access to your presentation. Open the folder where you saved your presentation (unzipped); you will see your "Index" page and an additional folder labeled DP. If you wish to view your portfolio, double-click on Index. A Web browser window will open and you can navigate your portfolio as if you were online! Burn both the index page and the Digital Portfolio folder to your CD-ROM if you wish to share your presentation with others.

You might also wish to download some or all the files in your File Cabinet. The directions are very similar to the downloading directions; the amount of time it will take depends on your connection speed and the number and size of files you wish to download.

Quick Clicks: Downloading the Files in Your File Cabinet

1. Go to the File Cabinet within your portfolio. First, select the individual files, or all the files, that you wish to download to your computer. To select a file, click on the box next to the filename. Or, you can select all the files in your file cabinet. At the bottom of the page, click on the **Select All** button (A).

2. When you have selected the files you wish to download, at the bottom of the page, click on **Download Selections** (B).

3. Once you click **Download Selections** you will get notification that the application is begriming to start the process.

4. Depending on the size of the files you are downloading, the process could be quick or take a few minutes. Be patient, you will be notified when to proceed.

5. Once the application has prepared your files, you will get a notification screen giving details about the download process.

6. You will be notified of the filename, the size, and estimated download times. This window must remain open during the entire process.

The next step is going to be deciding where to save the files on your local computer.

7. The **Save As** dialog box will automatically open for you. Here you can choose where to save the zipped file (A) and determine the file name for the folder (B). The file name will be pre-set by the portfolio application itself with your name. You can change the file name, but be sure to write down the new title and location where you are going to save.

8. After selecting a location to save and your file name, click **Save.** The downloading process will take a few moments, but you will be notified when it is complete.

9. The **Download Complete** dialog box will appear when your files have been completely saved onto your computer.

10. Click **Close.**

You have now saved your File Cabinet! You will see this type of icon with the filename in the site where you saved the zipped folder.

You have downloaded all of the files from your File Cabinet to your computer. They are saved in this zipped folder. Double-click on the icon to extract the files. (You will need an application to extract the files. Check to see if your computer has an unzip application installed by double-clicking on the filename.) Once you extract them, you have complete access to open, change, and view your files.

What If I Have a Problem?

If you have questions that are not answered in this manual, there are several options:

For Application-Related Issues

First, review the tutorial you viewed upon your initial login into the portfolio. This may answer any questions you have about beginning your portfolio. If you cannot find your answer there, then go to the integrated Help and FAQ (frequently asked questions) section of the online portfolio application. While logged into the portfolio, click on Help on the upper right-hand part of your screen. This comprehensive help site is frequently updated with new information based upon your feedback.

For Technical Issues

If you experience any type of technical problem, please do some basic troubleshooting. Check your computer's operation, your Internet connection, and the possible interference of any firewall or other security device. The portfolio is a Web-based application and it is highly unlikely that there would be a problem affecting only one or two users. While large-scale problems are possible, they are highly unlikely. The application is supported by a staff of professionals whose sole job is to keep it running smoothly for you. All data is backed up each night and there are redundant systems in place to maintain the highest quality of service for you.

Technical Support/Login and Password

If you have forgotten your user ID and/or password, go to **www.prenhall.com/jhuportfolio** and click the FAQ's tab on the navigation bar. You can also receive help with any Pearson product online at **http://247.prenhall.com** and via phone at 1-800-677-6337.